CONTENTS

BARRON'S PARENTING KEYS

KEYS TO PARENTING A CHILD WITH A LEARNING DISABILITY

Barry E. McNamara, Ed.D.,
and
Francine J. McNamara, M.S.W.,
C.S.W.

BARRON'S

Cover photo by Scott Barrow, Inc., Cold Spring, NY

DEDICATION
In loving memory of Dr. Joan Abrams. Her commitment to the education of all children was unsurpassed.

Credit line: Pages 113–115. From "ABC's of Homework: Tips for Parents" by J. B. Hodapp and A. F. Hodapp, *Intervention in School and Clinic, 26(5)*, 282–283. Copyright 1991 by PRO-ED, Inc. Reprinted by permission.

All inquiries should be addressed to:
Barron's Educational Series, Inc.
250 Wireless Boulevard
Hauppauge, New York 11788

Library of Congress Catalog Card No.: 95-112
International Standard Book No. 0-8120-9033-0

Library of Congress Cataloging-in-Publication Data
McNamara, Barry E., 1949–
   Keys to parenting a child with a learning disability / Barry E. McNamara and Francine J. McNamara.
      p.   cm. — (Barron's parenting keys)
   Includes bibliographical references and index.
   ISBN 0-8120-9033-0
   1. Learning disabled children—Education.   2. Education—Parent participation.   3. Home and school.   I. McNamara, Francine.   II. Title.   III. Series.
LC4704.73.M36   1995   95-112
371.91—dc20   CIP

PRINTED IN THE UNITED STATES OF AMERICA

   78   8800   98765432

INTRODUCTION

L*earning disability.* This term is thrown around a great deal lately. It seems like every problem a child has in school is labeled a learning disability. Why does a child diagnosed as learning disabled do some things so well and others so poorly? Why wasn't the school able to pick up the problem until the child was in the third grade? How did the parents miss signs of abnormal development or behavior before the child entered school? These and many more issues are raised when parents face the question, "Does my child have a learning disability?" Unfortunately, there are no clear-cut answers.

One thing we know for sure is that a wide variety of children can have these difficulties. For example, some pre-schoolers with learning disabilities may talk at an early age, others may not. Some walk at ten months, some not until age two. A delay in one area of development may not necessarily signal a problem. For that matter, "normal" development does not mean there is no learning disability. For these reasons, a learning disability may go undetected during the preschool years.

As children enter elementary school, such disabilities become easier to detect. Your son may not be able to concentrate in school and the teacher may ask you if anything is bothering him. Your daughter may not have the memory of other children her age, or you may notice her handwriting is illegible and she's having a hard time reading. As the problems continue, some children also develop behavioral or emotional disorders as a result of school failure. This is why early detection is critical. It is not surprising that students who enter high school with undetected learning disabilities are not motivated and have poor self-esteem. Some end up dropping out of school.

Nevertheless, there is good news: When parents and schools work together to identify and treat learning disabilities, students succeed. In fact, many of them go on to vocational programs or college after high school graduation.

This book provides parents of children with learning disabilities with the information necessary to be active partners with the school in helping their children. However, learning disabilities need to be addressed at home as well. Thus, this book also gives parents ways to help their child overcome learning disabilities outside school and in the community.

A successful partnership can only be achieved if parents are informed. This book allows parents to truly collaborate with professionals in the education of their children and to provide enriching experiences in the home and community.

Acknowledgments

We have received a great deal of support and encouragement from our publisher, specifically, Grace Freedson, Acquisitions Editor, and Linda Turner, our editor for this book and our previous book, *Keys to Parenting a Child with Attention Deficit Disorder*. Their concern and commitment to this project is greatly appreciated. We have been fortunate to have worked with such caring parents of children with learning disabilities. Their willingness to share their experiences with us enriched this book.

Finally, we want to acknowledge our daughters, Melissa and Tracy. The mere mention of their names brings a smile to our faces. They give meaning to all that we do.

Part One

WHAT IS A
LEARNING
DISABILITY?

Over the years an overwhelming number of definitions have been used to describe students with learning disabilities. Part one of this book defines the disorder so that parents will know exactly what a learning disability is and what it is not. After discussing issues related to the term's definition, the remaining keys focus on the causes and, more important, the major characteristics of the disabilities.

1

vvvvvvvvvvvvvvvvvvvvvvvvvvvvvvvvvvvvvvvvvvvvvvvvvvvv

LEARNING DISABILITIES DEFINED

Probably no other school-related classification has had as many definitions as *learning disabled*. Since the term was first used in the early 1960s it seemed like professionals were changing the definition every year. Parents of children with learning disabilities recognize how difficult it is to categorize the various difficulties their children encounter. The changes in definition came about because including or excluding some components caused concern and because the causes of learning disabilities weren't being addressed to the satisfaction of professionals.

Another issue that affected the term's definition was funding. How were schools going to pay for services for these students? Each definition tried to categorize those students termed learning disabled so that the group included those who required special education services and excluded those who didn't or who received other special education services. Those defining the term also wanted to ensure that it did not become a catchall for anyone who was simply having trouble in school.

The current definition used is cited in Public Law 101-476, *Individuals with Disabilities Education Act (IDEA)*, a federal law, which was passed in 1991. It states:

"Specific learning disability" means a disorder in one or more of the basic psychological processes involved in undertaking or in using language, spoken or written, which may manifest itself in an imperfect ability to listen, think, speak, read, write, spell, or to do mathematical calculations. The term includes such conditions as perceptual hardships, brain injury, minimal brain dysfunction, dyslexia and developmental apraxia. The term does not include children who have learning problems which are primarily the result of visual, hearing, or other hardships, of mental retardation, of emotional disturbance, or of environmental, cultural or economic disadvantage."

Basically the definition refers to students whose intellectual ability is above mental retardation and who show a discrepancy between potential and performance that cannot be explained in any other way. The last sentence of the definition, referred to as the exclusionary clause, has been widely criticized. Some experts in the field argue that it has been widely misinterpreted to mean that you cannot have other disabilities that coexist with learning disabilities. And although it may be difficult to determine the primary disability, almost all of the states employ this definition, including the exclusionary clause, for the identification of students with learning disabilities.

Beyond the exclusionary clause the definition has been criticized for a number of reasons: It is too broad; it focuses only on academic performance; it does not address the needs of adults; it leads to overidentification; and it ignores the needs of students with learning disabilities who live in multicultural, multiethnic, urban settings.

It is important to realize that this definition has been changed over the years and will continue to change as professionals and parents work together to serve the needs of individuals with learning disabilities. A different definition was suggested in 1990 by the National Joint Commission for Learning Disabilities. This is a group of nine professional organizations that works with individuals with learning disabilities. They define the disorder as follows:

> "Learning disabilities is a general term that refers to a heterogeneous group of disorders manifested by significant difficulties in the acquisition and use of listening, speaking, reading, writing, reasoning, or mathematical abilities. These disorders are intrinsic to the individual, presumed to be due to central nervous system dysfunction, and may occur across the life span. Problems in self-regulatory behavior, social perception, and social interaction may exist with learning disabilities but do not by themselves institute a learning disability. Although disabilities may occur concurrently with other handicapping conditions (for example, sensory impairment, mental retardation, serious emotional disturbance) or with extensive influences (such as cultural differences, insufficient or inappropriate understanding), they are not the result of those conditions or influences."

This definition addresses some of the criticisms of the federal definition. Still, new definitions will be formed and new criticisms will be found. Although these definitions may seem technical and confusing, parents must be aware of them because they provide the foundation for the referral, identification, and classification of students with learning disabilities.

2

~~~~~~

CHARACTERISTICS

Parents can feel overwhelmed by the long lists of characteristics of students with learning disabilities. This key addresses the major characteristics, which are then covered more fully in subsequent keys.

Motor Problems

Children and adolescents with learning disabilities may have trouble with tasks involving fine or gross motor skills. Fine motor tasks involve using such things as hands and fingers, whereas gross or large motor skills involve arm and leg movements or the larger muscles of the body. Students with learning disabilities may have trouble playing with blocks, puzzles, or beads, using a spoon, fork or knife, and coloring or copying shapes and objects. Their handwriting may be poor and they may have difficulty in activities that require coordination, such as gym, playground activities, and sports. Parents often say that their learning disabled child frequently bangs into objects, knocks things over, and is awkward.

Perceptual Deficits

Perceptual deficits can be divided into two major categories, auditory and visual. *Perception* is the interpretation of information that comes to us from our environment. If this information comes to us through our ears, it is referred to as *auditory perception*; if it comes to us through our eyes, it is referred to as *visual perception*.

Most information is not strictly visual or auditory, but rather a combination of the two. Students with learning disabilities have difficulty with different components of perception. For example, they may have trouble differentiating between letters that look alike (*b* for *d*, *w* for *m*) or words that are similar (*was* for *saw*), or being able to understand what someone is saying to you when there is a lot of noise in the room.

These are just a few of the problems a learning disabled child with a perceptual deficit might experience. Early in the study of learning disabilities many problems students encountered were attributed to their perceptual deficits. Subsequent research has not supported such contentions, yet it is clear that these deficits do exist for some students with learning disabilities.

Attention Deficits

It is estimated that approximately one-third of all students with learning disabilities have an Attention Deficit Disorder (ADD). Many other students with learning disabilities have other problems related to attention. ADD refers to a specific group of students who have difficulty concentrating on a task. They may or may not be hyperactive.

In order to diagnose this disorder a child or adolescent must undergo a thorough multidisciplinary evaluation, including assessment by a medical doctor (most often a neurologist). The treatment for ADD typically includes medication, counseling, and behavior management.

For the majority of students with learning disabilities, "attending" difficulties are related to the process one engages in learning. For example, they may have difficulty staying on task, deciding what is important and what is not in a lecture or reading passage, and they may not be able to sustain attention for particular tasks. This may not happen all the time—the way it does for students with ADD—but may be related to specific tasks. Many experts believe that many, if not most, students with learning disabilities have attention problems, but most (two-thirds) are not severe enough and do not occur often enough to be diagnosed as ADD.

Memory Disabilities

Some students who have learning disabilities have difficulty with memory. For some it is short term memory (STM). STM is, as the term suggests, short: it only lasts about 30 seconds. If you don't pay attention or *attend* to the information coming in from the environment you'll never get it into your short term memory. Clearly that is exactly what happens to many students with learning disabilities. If they attend and it goes into short term memory, it only lasts half a minute, so they need to do something with this information in order to get it into their long term memory (LTM). For example, you are introduced to someone at a party (STM) and you do nothing to remember the name; consequently, when you see this person the following week you have no idea of his name. However, if you did something to remember the name when you were introduced (STM), you would have been using what psychologists call *rehearsal*, and you would have a higher probability of committing it to your LTM and being able to retrieve it when you saw the person.

Memory is a complicated process that is not completely understood by researchers. However, it is clear that students with learning disabilities need assistance in using their memories. Parents of such students say things such as "he always forgets his keys," or "he never remembers to bring home his books," or they comment on how long their child studied, but still did not remember things on her test. All of these are related to memory function. Whether they represent a deficit in memory or how to use one's memory is not clear.

7

Language Disorders

Students with learning disabilities frequently have difficulty with the reception, processing, and expression of language. These problems appear to be persistent and continue through adulthood for about half of these students. Examples of difficulty with receptive language might include children who do not understand specific sounds, words, or sentences, or those that have difficulty understanding the structure of language. Receptive language problems always result in expressive language problems. If students do not understand what comes in, they will have problems expressing themselves (input precedes output). Some students with learning disabilities have trouble coming up with the correct words, frequently talking around something or describing it. Others may have trouble with the grammar of the language (syntax), that is they may not use the correct sequence of words or proper noun-verb agreement. And still others will have very little to comment on about the world in which they live. They tend to say very little spontaneously and even less upon demand.

Social Perceptual Disorders

Social perception can be defined as understanding the constraints of a social situation. For many students with learning disabilities this is a major problem.

Many parents notice that their child with a learning disability has a hard time making friends, says the wrong thing at the wrong time, does not think before he speaks, and says things most children don't say. These are just some of the characteristics of a child who has difficulty with social perceptual skills.

We probably know less about this area than other areas of deficit, but it may well be the most devastating because of its ramifications for the child or adolescent and his family.

Emotional Overlay

It is not surprising that emotional issues are closely related to having a learning disability. Children come to school wanting to succeed like everyone else. Children with learning disabilities often realize early in their school career that their best efforts don't always lead to success. Couple that with teachers and parents who may not recognize the disability, and it is obvious that undetected learning disabilities can lead to social-emotional difficulties.

Also, over the years people studying learning disabilities have concentrated on the academic aspects of the disorders. As a result, many students have carried the negative emotional baggage through adulthood.

These students do not have behavior disorders or significant emotional problems. (At least they didn't when they began their school career.) However, many professionals recognize that it does not take long before it is impossible to detect which disorder came first.

3

CAUSES AND PREVALENCE

The exact cause of a learning disability is unknown. This frustrates many parents who want to know "Why?" The problem with the research on causes is that there are so many things that can occur before (prenatal), during (perinatal), or after (postnatal) birth that it is virtually impossible to pinpoint when the difficulty begins. Moreover, there are children who have experienced considerable difficulty during these stages and have emerged without any school related problems.

Two possible causes that have often been cited in the professional literature are Central Nervous System Disorder and genetic factors.

Central Nervous System Disorder

A number of before birth or prenatal factors have been cited as being associated with learning disabilities: baby/mother blood incompatibility, inborn errors of metabolism, age of mother, number of pregnancies, drug and alcohol abuse, smoking, medication, fetal infection, low birth weight, and prematurity.

During the birth process nervous system damage may occur because of oxygen deprivation, the type of labor, or any agent that makes birth difficult. Obviously head injuries can occur throughout the life span and they along with strokes, high fever, and disease can cause a Central Nervous System Disorder. However, this type of disorder does not necessarily mean there will be a learning disability.

Genetic Factors

More and more evidence suggests an association between learning disabilities and genetic factors. Professionals readily point to cases where learning disabilities run in families, and some research supports this observation. Twin studies point to the influences of genetics on learning disabilities, showing that learning disabilities are found more frequently in identical twins than in fraternal twins. Obviously, important environmental components need to be explored as well. However, the role of genetics cannot be dismissed.

A learning disability is most likely related to a central nervous system disfunction of unknown origin. Fortunately, researchers continue to explore causes in the hope that the more knowledge will foster prevention of learning disabilities.

Not being able to attribute a learning disability to a specific cause can lead parents to try a wide variety of controversial treatments that attempt to "cure" a learning disability. The search for the cause can delay appropriate intervention. Energy is better spent on what parents and schools can do to circumvent the learning disability and provide children with compensatory strategies.

Prevalence

How many students have learning disabilities? Some say the range is as low as 1-2 percent, and others say it is as large as 40 percent! Three to 5 percent seems to be the percentage most often cited. This is a relatively small percentage of the school-aged population, yet it is highly publicized in the media. This may be due to the fact that in many school districts the majority of students classified with any disability are put in the learning disabled category. In some parts of the country this category may account for 80 percent of all students classified as having a disability. However, nationally the percentage of special education students who are classified as learning disabled is around 50 percent.

Boys outnumber girls in programs for learning disabilities by as much as three to one and four to one.

A number of reasons have been suggested for this phenomenon. Boys are more vulnerable to prenatal brain injury and such injury during the birth process, which may place them at risk for learning disabilities. Boys' neurological development may also be more vulnerable during the prenatal period.

Socio-cultural reasons are also cited. Expectations for boys and girls differ in schools where the majority of teachers are female. Parental expectations for traditional male and female roles may affect performance. The nature of sexual inequity in schools, whereby girls don't always receive the same types of services that boys do may also be a contributing factor.

Many professionals feel that schools treat males and females very differently. They suggest that boys receive more teacher attention and are provided with more opportunities. They also think that because of this boys are provided with more special services in schools because it's important for them to succeed. These are not the only reasons why boys outnumber girls in programs for learning disabled students, but they cannot be ignored.

4

MOTOR AND PERCEPTUAL PROBLEMS

Early researchers in the field of learning disabilities believed that motor learning (walking, hopping, jumping, throwing, etc.) was a prerequisite to high level learning, such as talking, reading, and writing. In order to communicate, read, and write a child must be proficient in motor learning. Therefore, in the 60s and early 70s many educational programs resembled what we now call adaptive physical education. That is, they focused on motor activities such as hopping, skipping, jumping, throwing, catching, obstacle courses and the like.

The thinking was that these skills had to be learned by students in order for them to progress to other more academically oriented skills. Research conducted in the early 70s did not support this. And while some people continue to espouse this approach, current theories in the field do not support the use of isolated training in motor or perceptual-motor activities.

This does not mean that students with learning disabilities do not have motor problems. Many parents report that their children are awkward or clumsy, or that they were delayed in walking or riding a bike. Others will tell you that their children are always bumping into things, have a hard time with sports, and do not enjoy physical activities. Teachers often note that these students have a hard time with handwriting, cutting with scissors, buttoning a coat, or tying a shoelace. They may not be able to catch a ball, or perhaps they drop their books, and they never play with anyone on the playground.

Clearly learning disabled students have motor problems. What has changed over the years is our approach to remedy them. For a child with a motor problem, multifaceted intervention now might include adaptive physical education in order to modify the existing physical education program and meet the individual needs of the student; occupational therapy to increase the student's fine motor skills; or physical therapy to work on the student's gross motor skills.

Students with motor problems may become easily frustrated because they cannot express what they have learned. They often write little because writing is so difficult. Their handwriting can be sloppy and illegible. This can also cause difficulty with mathematics. Because of the misalignment and illegibility of the numbers they write, they make mistakes.

What about the child or adolescent who is not well coordinated and does poorly in physical activities? Many parents tell tales of woe about their child being the target of taunts because they are not good in sports. The rejection and isolation affects not just the child but the entire family. Some children show motor problems at an early age, and so it is clear that later on their performance in specific games and activities will be hindered. With other children it is not so clear.

In any case, parents must be alert to the motor component of learning and ensure that their child receives appropriate treatment. Also, the selection of some activities and modification of others is crucial.

Children with spacial relation problems have trouble sequencing letters in words and words in sentences. They may also have trouble walking through a crowded classroom or store without knocking things over. *Visual discrimination* is the ability to distinguish one object from another. A typical example of this would be students who reverse letters (*b* for *d*, *p* for *q*) or words (*was* for *saw*).

Figure-ground discrimination is the ability to distinguish an object from the background. Students struggling with this skill may also have trouble concentrating on one word or tracing objects when there are overlapping objects. Focusing on important information on the blackboard when there is a lot written on the board may be difficult, too.

Visual closure is the ability to identify the whole when only a part is shown. Activities in children's workbooks where they have to find all the socks or all the fish exercise this skill. The child looks through and has to identify the correct number of items even though only parts of them can be seen. A child with a visual closure problem would have difficulty with this activity. Identifying a word when it is partially covered would also be difficult. Finally, children with visual memory problems may have trouble identifying letters, numbers, and words as well as shapes and objects.

Auditory perceptual problems can be divided into auditory discrimination, auditory figure-ground, auditory memory, and auditory blending. Auditory discrimination is the ability to distinguish similarities and differences between sounds. Students with auditory discrimination problems have a hard time following directions and have problems with all aspects of phonics. Students with difficulty in auditory figure-ground cannot identify the major source of the information they are hearing from the background. Teachers may comment that "he knows exactly what is going on all around him, but does not hear a word I say." Parents often repeat that they "listen to everything but what they are supposed to listen to." These students cannot distinguish the relevant from the irrelevant in a lecture or conversation. An auditory memory problem will manifest itself in the inability to recall information the child has heard. These children may have trouble recalling the days of the week, a phone number, and sequences of words, as well as commands (especially if there is more than one). Many children with learning disabilities have difficulty blending the isolated sounds of words together. This skill, called auditory blending, is critical for success if a child is being taught through a phonics-based approach. It is less of an issue if other approaches are employed.

As was the case with motor problems, leaders in the field of learning disabilities felt that these skills were critical for future success. Once again, this was not supported by research. To say that students with learning disabilities do not have perceptual problems is naive. However, it is clear that isolated remediation of perceptual processes is ineffective. How motor and perceptual problems affect academic performance must be the focus of understanding students with learning disabilities.

5

ATTENTION DEFICIT DISORDERS

What is Attention Deficit Disorder (ADD)? The term has been renamed and redefined by various disciplines over the years. In the 1960s a child with an attention problem evaluated by a physician would most likely have been labeled as having *minimal brain dysfunction* (MBD). The school might have used the term *learning disabled* or *hyperactive*. Currently, the term most frequently employed is *Attention Deficit Hyperactivity Disorder* (ADHD). Experts suggest using the more general term *Attention Deficit Disorder* (ADD) because it includes any kind of attentional problem, not just those involving hyperactivity.

Commonly cited characteristics of children with ADD are hyperactivity, distractibility, and impulsivity. They have difficulty staying on task and focusing on important aspects of conversations or school-related tasks. Frequently they do not complete tasks because they are moving rapidly from one activity to another or are distracted by extraneous stimuli. Parents say these children require little sleep, are very restless, and are constantly in motion.

Hyperactivity is a specific central nervous system disorder that makes it difficult for children to control their motor activity. These children may not be constantly on the go, but they appear restless and fidgety. Parents may say their child can't sit through a meal, moves from one activity to another very rapidly, or "never shuts up." Teachers describe these students as always doing something. They often get up to sharpen their pencil, tap their pencil or their fingers on the desk, or tap their foot on the floor. They finish assignments quickly and often incorrectly, run around on the playground or squirm at their desks.

These behaviors often have no purpose or focus. An observer may say "I don't know where he gets his energy" or "I wish I had his energy." Yet this is not the type of energy that allows someone to accomplish a great deal. Quite the opposite, it interferes with productivity. The term *hyperactive* is overused. Many children and adolescents should not be referred to as hyperactive. The term should not be used casually, but reserved for those children and adolescents with the specific disorder. Without a multidisciplinary evaluation, including a medical evaluation, it is difficult to judge a child's movements as hyperactive.

Some children may not be hyperactive but may have great difficulty staying on task. These children are easily distracted and struggle to filter information that comes in via the senses. Most people can block out certain bits of information from the environment and focus on what is important. Unfortunately, children who are distractible are not good at discriminating between relevant and irrelevant information, thus everything competes for their attention. They are unable to focus on a specific task for a long period of time, thus the term *short attention span* is often used to describe them.

Children and adolescents who are easily distracted can be bothered by a slight noise in another part of the room. They may hear someone talking outside the house and be distracted by it. A car goes by the window and they rush to look out. They may walk into the bedroom to get something, their attention shifts to a picture on the wall, and they forget why they went into the bedroom. Many of these children experience difficulty in places where a great deal is going on, such as birthday parties, shopping malls, and carnivals. They can become irritable and restless because of increased stimulation in their surroundings. Some classrooms can cause the same problem when so much is going on that the child can't attend effectively.

Some children with ADD are impulsive. They act first and think later. They may say things that are offensive, but not realize it until it is pointed out to them. A youngster may even hit his classmates frequently and then apologize profusely. He is unable to anticipate the meaning of his behavior and he merely acts out. Impulsive children ask questions that have nothing to do with the conversation at hand. In class, these children call out answers before the questions have been asked (and they are usually the wrong answers). Such impulsive children and adolescents appear to be accident prone because they do not attend to the consequences of their actions. Children like this have jumped out of windows, fallen out of trees, and run through glass doors. Many get an incredible number of cuts, scratches, and bruises. The behavior of the child who truly has ADD will be manifested in both school and home. If a child only displays these characteristics in one such setting, then it can probably be attributed to causes other than ADD.

About two-thirds of students with learning disabilities, while not as severe or pervasive as ADD, still display behaviors associated with attention problems. For example, many students with learning disabilities have a difficult time determining important from unimportant material. They will study for hours, only to do poorly on an exam because they studied the wrong things. Students with learning disabilities sometimes claim that teachers tricked them on tests; they don't recognize that teachers provided many clues as to what was important.

Parents and teachers comment that children or adolescents with learning disabilities have limited attention spans. In fact, when teachers are asked to cite characteristics of students with learning disabilities, short attention span and hyperactivity are high on the list.

6

MEMORY DISORDERS

All teachers and parents of children with learning disabilities say the children have problems with memory. They often remark "she forgets everything," or "If I don't remind her, she never remembers," or "when I mention something we discussed for an entire week she looks at me like she doesn't have a clue about what I'm talking about."

It seems like these children and adolescents just forget. Perhaps, but it is not so simple. Memory is a complex process that involves much more than the number of things a person can remember. Memory encompasses knowing what needs to be remembered, strategies for remembering, and learning to access information that you stored in your memory bank. Knowing how your memory works can help you use it more efficiently.

Some people have excellent memories. They seem to be gifted. In some cases they are. Most people, however, employ a number of strategies that enable them to use their memories effectively and efficiently. The ability to understand the demand of the task, to know what strategies to use, to use them effectively, and to learn how to retrieve information may be at the core of the problem for students with learning disabilities. A visual model will help explain this process.

Environment	Short-Term Memory	Long-Term Memory

Information comes to us through the environment. If a child has a perceptual processing disorder, this information may be compounded and affect memory functioning. If there is no problem interpreting the information (perception) then the child must attend to the information in order for it to get into the short-term memory. If a child or adolescent has an Attention Deficit Disorder, memory functioning will definitely be hindered. So it is clear that many children and adolescents with learning disabilities do not even get information into their short-term memory. They don't forget it, they never had the opportunity (or strategy or process) to remember it.

Once information gets into short-term memory something must be done in order to get it into long-term memory. Short-term memory is often used incorrectly. A teacher might say, "We covered this all last week, and on Monday they forget it completely. They have short-term memory." Even some adults comment, "I just read about that yesterday and I can't remember it. I have a terrible short-term memory." Neither is an accurate statement about short-term memory.

Short-term memory is very short, possibly only about 30 seconds. So if you don't do anything with the information to be remembered, it will be lost. In order for information to proceed to long-term memory (some refer to this as long-term memory storage) you must act upon the information or "rehearse" it.

For example, you are introduced to someone you don't think you will ever see again, so you don't do anything to remember his name. Then you end up running into him the next week and you cannot recall his name. If you had thought of a way to remember the name, however, such as associating a characteristic with the first letter of the name or associating his face with someone of a similar name, then you would probably remember it.

In school settings students with learning disabilities are required to recall information far more complex than someone's name, but the process is the same. They must act on the information in order for it to go into long-term memory and be retrievable at a later date.

For students with learning disabilities a breakdown can occur anywhere in the memory process. Many times they are unaware that they need a strategy in order to remember. They also are less likely to be introspective and aware of their own difficulties. Instead of trying to compensate for their inability to remember, try to teach them strategies to help them remember. For example, if they cannot remember their homework, teach them to write it down in a special notebook. If they always misplace their keys, have them find a place in the house where they can *always* put them. These strategies can be taught and some promising findings indicate that when students with learning disabilities learn how to employ specific strategies their ability to learn improves.

Memory is a complex task, involving much more than the rapid recall of facts and figures. It is a developmental process that involves the ability to attend to, perceive, organize, store, and retrieve information. The problems that learning disabled students have with memory may involve any or all of the parts of memory as well as the complexity of the information they have to remember.

7

LANGUAGE DISORDERS

A language disorder may be the most pervasive of all the characteristics of students with learning disabilities. It can cause difficulties in all areas of the curriculum. A student with an oral language disorder will have difficulty learning to read, and a student who has trouble reading will have written language disorders.

Oral Language

Students with learning disabilities may have difficulty understanding language (referred to as oral receptive language) or difficulty communicating with others (oral expressive language). There is a close relationship between receptive and expressive language.

Some children with learning disabilities don't recognize familiar sounds and don't understand simple questions. They may not be able to understand simple stories or respond to simple requests. As they get older, they may struggle to understand more complex stories that are read to them, and they may have a difficult time following more than one command. Their oral expressive language may be delayed, and they may stay at the one-word stage for a longer period of time than most children. Many parents of learning disabled children report that the children said their first word around 12 months of age, but did not start to put words together ("more milk" or "want cookie") until three years of age.

Oral expressive language disorders include "word finding" problems, apraxia, and disorders of formulation and syntax. All of these are described in this key.

When a child or adolescent knows the word, but cannot recall it for spontaneous usage, she has a "word finding" problem. (The terms *dysnomia* or *word retrieval problem* are also used to describe this disorder.) Some people call this the tip-of-the-tongue phenomenon. It has happened to all of us, but it happens much more to some people with learning disabilities.

For example, a child might tell you about a ride in her car and say, "Yesterday we took a ride in the [pause] the thing you drive, you know, it has four wheels [makes a gesture of steering the car], goes fast, you know." If shown a picture of a car the child would be able to identify it without problem, he just can't retrieve the word when he needs it in order to communicate.

Other children or adolescents may have a disorder called *apraxia*. Apraxia is a disorder that affects the muscles used to speak, without causing paralysis. There is nothing physically wrong with the mouth, teeth, or tongue that would prevent the child from being able to produce sounds and words correctly, but the child is still unable to do so. The condition is probably due to a central nervous system disorder. These children are difficult to understand, and over time the frustration of not being able to communicate may cause emotional problems.

Formulation of syntax disorders affect the ability to freely express ideas through oral language and to produce grammatically correct phrases and sentences. Children and adolescents with learning disabilities may have problems with pronoun usage, noun-verb agreement, and word order. A student may ask, "What multiplication is?" Or in response to the question "What is your name?," a young child with learning disabilities may say "John am I."

25

Written Expressive Language

Children with handwriting difficulty find writing a chore. It takes a great deal of time and effort. Imagine how you would feel if you walked into a classroom and the board was filled with notes you were required to copy. The typical learner may just sigh and moan at the task. For the student who has a learning disability in writing, it can be disastrous.

So much effort goes into the formulation, position, and spacing of the letters that the student cannot even focus on anything else. Some students hold the pencil incorrectly, usually with a very high tight grasp. Other students will do anything to get out of these writing tasks, including acting out in class so they can be removed to the principal's office. For them it is better to be punished for inappropriate behavior than having to struggle through an activity where failure is inevitable.

It is no wonder that these students struggle so much to communicate through writing when the act of writing is so painful. They cannot concentrate on their ideas or the subject matter because they are so focused on the actual task of writing.

Even when handwriting does not pose a problem children and adolescents with learning disabilities have considerable trouble with written expression. Typically, they generate less thoughtful writing samples, more simplistic vocabulary than expected, and they cannot develop a theme or main idea in a composition. Teachers often say that these students cannot understand the concept of a story's beginning, middle, and end. Research in this area suggests that these students write fewer words, fewer sentences, and have fewer ideas than their classmates.

8

SOCIAL PERCEPTUAL DISORDERS

I n the early development of the field of learning disabilities, the emphasis was on the identification of process disorders (perception, attention, memory, cognition) and academic disorders (reading, writing, spelling, and mathematics). Then for over two decades parents told teachers that in addition to learning problems, their children had no friends or related better to younger children. The children always seemed to say the wrong thing at the wrong time. These parents saw that learning disabilities went way beyond academics. They affected the social and emotional development of their children.

Professionals came to the same realization and recognized that many (surely not all) individuals had difficulty getting along with others and understanding the constraints of social situations. This disorder is known as a social perceptual disorder. While it is not as pervasive as some of the other characteristics it causes considerable problems for the children or adolescents and their families.

Some very simple social interactions can be disastrous for these children. For example, they may have difficulty interpreting facial expressions and body language. They may not know if the individual they are interacting with is happy, sad, or angry based on the way they look. This coupled with language disorders can lead to very difficult social interaction.

Most nondisabled students at one time may act silly in a classroom, and unless the teacher tells them to stop, they stop on their own. However, the student with a learning disability is unable to understand when enough is enough and may continue to act out until being removed from the class.

Many students with learning disabilities feel they are always getting picked on at home and at school. When they explain the situation, it is usually apparent that the teacher or parent gave ample opportunities for the child to stop the inappropriate behavior. It is also obvious that the child didn't recognize these opportunities at all. The ability to understand such social situation is impaired. Parents often describe similar situations and comment, "He doesn't know when to stop."

This inability to interpret social situations goes beyond facial expressions and body language. The individuals may lack the ability to understand the nature of the setting, the expectations of the individual or group they are working with or socializing with, and most likely will not appreciate the underlying and subtle attitudes that are conveyed through social interactions.

Children and adolescents with this disorder are often negatively portrayed as egocentric—thinking only of themselves. It may be their inability to put themselves in someone else's position that makes them appear to be so self-centered. When confronted, they are perplexed that others view them this way.

Learning disabled students often say exactly what they think, before considering the consequences of their remarks. Teachers and parents cite many examples of such comments that were at least inappropriate ("You really think that tie goes with that shirt?") to outright hurtful ("Your yearbook picture is ugly!"). The important point is that this is not done maliciously. Children without the disability would understand that these comments would hurt someone's feelings. As a peer of a student with learning disabilities once remarked, "I think about the things she says, but I don't say them."

Parents of children with learning disabilities often remark that they can keep no secrets. Their children often do not realize that some comments made at home are best kept at home and that some things said in exasperation probably should not be shared with others. For example, a family was taking a long vacation by car and stopped at the home of one of the grandparents. It was not a convenient detour, and apparently the mother was complaining in the car about having to stop at the in-laws. When they arrived at the house the mother mentioned how nice it was to see her mother-in-law. Her 10-year-old son with a learning disability blurted out, "That's not what you were saying in the car!"

These children may also have a difficult time expressing their needs and may not understand that just blurting out what they want is not appropriate. One parent shared the following story, which exemplifies this problem. Their family went to a fairly crowded coffee shop for lunch. The child ordered a sandwich. When the waitress brought his sandwich to the table he noticed packets of mustard on the plate and screamed, "I hate mustard on pastrami!" He startled the poor waitress so that she dropped the entire order. Naturally, everyone in the restaurant turned to look at the commotion, his parents looked at him in disgust, and he said meekly, "You know I hate mustard." He did not know the socially appropriate way to indicate displeasure. As a result, his parents are reluctant to have him in certain social settings.

29

Social perceptual disorders can be more debilitating than academic disorders to learning disabled individuals. The disorders impair the ability to make friends, they limit opportunities for socialization, and make the child the target of verbal reprimands from parents and teachers alike. Many adults find it impossible to understand how such bright children could say such things.

One teacher could never understand why a student in his seventh grade English class once did the following: Two students with learning disabilities, Maria and Sara, were in the class. They were friends. Maria was hurt in school and had to be hospitalized. During class, the teacher told Sara, "Say hello to Maria when you visit the hospital and tell her I hope she feels better." The following day during English class the teacher asked Sara if she told this to Maria. When she said "yes," he asked what Maria had said. "She told me to tell you to mind your own business." (Expletives deleted.). The class erupted in laughter. The teacher turned bright red and glared at Sara, who merely said, "That's what Maria said." Sara did not understand that it was not a good idea to repeat those remarks.

9

ACADEMIC DISORDERS

For many students the first indication that there is a learning disability occurs when they attend school. Surely there are signs of a learning disability before this time. But it is usually not until a child reaches school age that it becomes clear that the problems he or she has are more than immaturity, inattentiveness, or whatever term was used to describe the child's behavior. In fact, many people have criticized the classification of "learning disability" as only a school-related disorder.

Learning processes, such as perception, attention, memory, and language, are involved in a variety of academic disorders. Students with learning disabilities may have difficulty in all school subjects, but they are most often referred for an evaluation due to problems in reading. Reports in professional literature note that about 85 percent of the students who are classified as learning disabled are classified as such due to reading problems. Others have argued that this high percentage is due to an overemphasis on literacy as opposed to proficiency in mathematics or other areas. Whatever the reason, the majority of students who receive special education services due to being classified as learning disabled are having trouble reading.

Other children with learning disabilities have difficulties with attending to a task or have Attention Deficit Disorder, which may affect their ability to read. The same can be said for memory disorders. That is, the disorder in the memory process underlying learning usually manifests itself in an academic disorder. This has led to much confusion over the years about how to remediate various learning disabilities. Specifically, should teachers remediate the process (perception, memory, etc.) or the academic skill area (reading, writing, etc.)?

Although there has been considerable debate on this, most research suggests remediation of the academic skill, with an understanding of the underlying process disorder. For example, a child with a visual perceptual problem may struggle with long division. It is hard for many people to keep track of each step and make sure the problem is properly aligned. The student with a visual perceptual problem may find this impossible without assistance. The teacher may reduce the number of problems on the page, color code the steps, and teach specific memory strategies—all of which are designed so that the child has the ability to do the problem if the perceptual deficit is addressed. This is very different from doing isolated perceptual training exercises that have nothing to do with the academic area.

Other academic areas that pose problems to students with learning disabilities are spelling, penmanship, and written expressive language. Experts in the field of learning disabilities have noted that written expressive language (i.e. putting your thoughts into writing) is the most difficult skill to remediate. In fact, it is not unusual to see intelligent college students with learning disabilities continue to struggle with written expression throughout their academic careers. Of course, many students not termed learning disabled have similar difficulty with written expression.

Students with learning disabilities can have difficulty with mathematics. However, as mentioned, less emphasis is placed on these problems in mathematics than in other areas. Too often children with disorders receive little help, are placed in less demanding courses, and develop a dislike or even a fear of math. This is unfortunate because if more equity was given to math instruction for students with learning disabilities, more options would be available to them as they advanced through the grades.

As they advance, students with learning disabilities continue to have difficulty with basic skills in other content areas (general studies, science, etc.). They may struggle with vocabulary and higher level thinking skills necessary for such learning. Moreover, they usually lack the strategies necessary for success in the content areas.

Success in school is not solely related to proficiency in academic skills. The quality of interaction between teacher and student as well as the school-related behaviors the student engages in reflect school performance. For many students with learning disabilities, particularly adolescents, academic disorders are often made worse by social perceptual problems.

Part Two

~~~~~~

DIAGNOSIS OF A LEARNING DISABILITY

How do you know if the difficulties your child is having are due to a learning disability? There are many reasons why children and adolescents have problems in school, learning disabilities only being one of them. The way to find out if your child has a learning disability is to have her evaluated. Part Two provides parents with the information they need to get an evaluation and to understand it.

10

WHAT TO DO IF YOU SUSPECT A LEARNING DISABILITY

The National Information Center for Children and Youth with Disabilities (NICHCY), located in Washington, DC, distributes information on a variety of services for special education. Some common questions and answers adapted from an NICHCY bulletin about how to proceed if you suspect a learning disability are outlined in this key. One of the purposes of assessment is to identify the specific disability. These steps are appropriate to take for any disability.

What is the first step to take if I suspect my child has a learning disability and may need special education services?

The first step is to arrange for your child to receive an assessment. The term *assessment* refers to the total process of gathering and using information to make decisions about your child's educational needs. The public schools are required to provide an assessment for your child at no cost to you. The assessment process should look at the "whole child" and include information about your child's total environment.

Information gathered from formal tests, along with observations provided by school personnel and you, the parents, will form the basis for your child's Individualized Education Program (IEP). The IEP will describe learning goals for your child and will note the services that the school district will be required to provide for your child.

What is included in an assessment?

Tests are an important part of an assessment, but your input into the assessment process is also vital. In addition to testing, the assessment process should include the following:

- observations by professionals who have worked with your child;
- your child's medical history, when it is relevant to his performance in school; and
- your information and observations about your child's school experiences, abilities, needs, and behavior outside of school, and his feelings about school.

The team conducting the assessment may include the following professionals:

- school psychologist;
- speech and language therapist;
- occupational therapist;
- physical therapist or adaptive physical education therapists;
- medical specialists;
- educational diagnosticians;
- learning disability teacher; and
- classroom teachers.

Professionals will observe your child and may administer tests that examine the following:

- speech and language functioning;
- personality and adaptive behavior patterns;

- academic achievements;
- potential or aptitude (intelligence);
- functioning levels (how they are performing in the classroom);
- perceptual ability; and
- vocational interest and aptitude.

All tests must be given to your child individually in his primary language, and in a way that does not discriminate on the basis of disability or racial/cultural background.

No one test may be used as the only basis of your child's assessment. Many tests are needed to measure areas that may be problematic. The law does not require that one specific test be used, and many tests measure the same thing. A specialist may choose a certain test as long as the test measures what the specialist says it will measure and is considered to be nondiscriminatory.

How can my child receive an assessment?

There are at least three ways in which your child may be selected to receive an assessment:

1. **You can request an assessment.** You can call or write the Director of Special Education or the Principal of your child's school. When an assessment is requested by a parent, the school must reply in writing within 30 days. If the school refuses to assess your child, you must be given a written notice that explains reasons for the refusal. This notice must also give you a full explanation of your rights under The Individuals with Disabilities Education Act (IDEA). IT IS VERY IMPORTANT THAT YOU KEEP A COPY OF THIS LETTER, IN ADDITION TO ALL CORRESPONDENCE THAT YOU HAVE RECEIVED ABOUT YOUR CHILD.

2. **The school may ask permission to assess your child.** A school may recommend a child for screening or assessment based on observations or results from tests given to all children in a grade. If your child needs further testing, the school must tell you. You, as a parent, must give written permission before the school can schedule an assessment for your child.

3. **A teacher may suggest that your child be assessed.** Your child's teacher may recommend that your child have an assessment. Again, you must give permission in writing before the school can conduct the assessment.

All screening and assessment procedures scheduled, arranged, or conducted by the school system are to be done at no cost to you. If your child's assessment is conducted by a specialist outside of the school, it is necessary for the school to make arrangements and state in writing the extent of the assessment for which it will pay. If the outside specialist recommends further testing once the assessment has begun, contact the school to obtain its commitment to be responsible for the expanded assessment.

When should I consider obtaining an independent evaluation for my child?

The purpose of an independent evaluation is to obtain a second professional opinion. If you believe that the school's assessment is inaccurate or incomplete, you may request an outside evaluation. Arrangements to have an independent evaluation must be made through the school if the school system is expected to pay for it.

Additionally, you may arrange to have your child independently evaluated at any time if the school system is not expected to pay for the evaluation. No matter who pays for the outside evaluation, if it is conducted by an appropriately cre-dentialed specialist, the information may be used in a hearing to determine your child's educational program. If a hearing officer requests an independent evaluation, the school district must pay for it. You may find a specialist to conduct an outside evaluation from the following sources:

- your child's school district, which must provide you with the names of professionals in the community;
- parent groups, which can provide you with recommendations of professionals they have found helpful; and
- local hospitals and universities, which can provide you with the names of physical therapists, occupational therapists, speech and language therapists, educational diagnosticians, and other medical specialists.

Above all it is very important for schools and parents to work together in order to help children. The steps outlined here are best undertaken in a spirit of cooperation, not adversity. The goal is to ensure that the needs of the student with learning disabilities are met.

11

‸‸

THE MULTIDISCIPLINARY EVALUATION

It is not easy to diagnose a learning disability; information must be gathered from a variety of sources. The evaluation should be done by a group of professionals, referred to as a multidisciplinary team. This team may consist of a psychologist, a special educator, and a social worker. They work together in making a diagnosis that will provide you with a total picture.

A **psychologist** will evaluate the intellectual and socio-emotional functioning of a child. The psychologist will look for emotional disturbances or other psychological disorders that may exist with a learning disability or may be the main problem.

A **special educator**, thoroughly trained in psycho-educational assessment procedures, will explore the existence of a learning disability or other school-related disorders. The student will be assessed in basic psychological processes (attention, memory, perception) and basic skill subjects (reading, math, and so on) in order to determine specific strengths and weaknesses. The assessment procedures may vary from state to state.

The **social worker** will meet with the family to obtain information about the child's social history including birth information, developmental milestones, family dynamics, medical information, and school placement.

Your child's regular education teacher will be asked to provide information about classroom performance and behavior, and to document interventions that have been tried in the regular classroom.

In the case of learning disabilities, it may be necessary for additional evaluation by other professionals, such as a speech and language specialist, a physical therapist, or an occupational therapist.

By collecting information from a variety of sources there is less of a chance of misdiagnosis. Many professionals believe that learning disabilities are overdiagnosed. That is, anyone who has any kind of trouble in school would be classified as "LD." A multidisciplinary approach helps reduce such misdiagnosis because other reasons for the school problem could be discovered. For example, the child may be having trouble in school because of family difficulties, low intellectual abilities, or a significant language disorder.

When all professionals have accumulated their findings, a meeting is held to discuss their results, to determine the existence or absence of a learning disability, and to develop an IEP.

The following keys in Part Two will provide more specific information on each component of the multidisciplinary evaluation.

12

PSYCHOLOGICAL EVALUATION

T he psychological evaluation should be done by a doctoral level, licensed psychologist, who is either a clinical or school psychologist.

The psychologist will administer an individual intelligence test, usually referred to as an I.Q. (Intelligence Quotient) test. An individually administered test is very different from standardized, group administered tests. The group administered tests usually require children to write their response on an answer sheet. An individually administered test is given to one child. Most questions require verbal responses or that the child do something, but there is little or no writing or reading.

A number of intelligence tests are available to the psychologist, who should select the most appropriate test based on the student's needs. For example, if a child has speech and language problems, a test would be selected that does not require the student to talk. If English is not the child's native language another type of test may be selected. Generally, the two most popular individually administered intelligence tests are the Stanford-Binet Intelligence Scale and the Wechsler Scales.

- *The Stanford-Binet Intelligence Scale*, for children age two through adulthood, provides a mental age that can be converted into an I.Q. score. Although it presents items that require verbal and nonverbal performance, it has many more verbal items; thus, the Wechsler Scales are used more often.

- *The Wechsler Pre-School and Primary Scale of Intelligence (WPPSI)* is used for students who are four to six and a half years old. This test measures a child's verbal skills, nonverbal reasoning abilities, and perceptual motor skills.
- *The Wechsler Intelligence Scales for Children-III (WISC-III)* is used for students age six through 16. Some psychologists use The Wechsler Intelligence Scales for Children—Revised (WISC-R). However, the most recent test (WISC-III) has parts that are helpful in the diagnosis of ADD. Also, the standardized procedures are more up-to-date. It measures verbal and nonverbal performance skills (five parts for each).
- *The Wechsler Adult Intelligence Scales (WAIS)* is used with adolescents and adults. This test is intended for ages 16 through adulthood and measures verbal and nonverbal performance abilities.

If your child is school age, the WISC-III or the WISC-R will probably be the test that is given. For many parents the concept of I.Q. is mysterious. To give you a sense of what these tests measure, we will discuss the WISC because it is used so often.

The test is divided into ten parts: five verbal and five performance. When evaluating the results of this test the psychologist is looking for overall potential to learn. The WISC yields three scores: Verbal I.Q., Performance I.Q., and Full-Scale I.Q. The average I.Q. falls between 90 and 110.

The Verbal Scale of the WISC includes the following areas:

- **Information** This measures how much general information the child has learned from school and home.
- **Comprehension** This measures how well your child can think abstractly and understand concepts.
- **Similarities** This also measures the child's ability to think abstractly. Children tell how things are alike or different.

43

- **Arithmetic** This is not paper and pencil arithmetic. Rather it measures verbal mathematical reasoning skills by giving the child oral problems to solve.
- **Vocabulary** Children tell what a word means by explaining or defining it. A dictionary definition is not necessary.
- **Digit Span** This measures a child's ability to remember a sequence of numbers (forward and backward). This subtest is optional and does not have to be included.

The Performance Scale of the WISC includes the following areas:

- **Picture Completion** Children have to look at pictures and tell the examiner what part is missing.
- **Picture Arrangement** This requires a child to put pictures in order so that the story makes sense. It measures their ability to create the whole when only the parts are given.
- **Block Design** Unlike picture arrangement where children are given the parts and make up the whole, this test measures the child's ability to look at the whole first, then break it into parts, and finally to reconstruct the whole. It provides blocks and pictures, and the child must put the blocks together to recreate what's in the picture of the blocks.
- **Object Assembly** The child is given puzzle parts and must complete the puzzle. It measures a child's ability to make a whole out of its parts.
- **Coding** This section measures a child's ability to decipher a code and copy the correct symbols in a specific period of time.
- **Mazes** The child has to find the way out of a maze by using a pencil. Performance is also based on time.

In addition to measuring intelligence, the psychologist will look at behavioral and social-emotional functioning. She may use specific tests, interviewing techniques or rating scales to do so.

13

EDUCATIONAL
EVALUATION

A thorough educational evaluation, sometimes referred to as a pyschoeducational evaluation, will provide you with your child's educational strengths, weaknesses, and recommendations for educational interventions.

No special certification or license is usually required of the person who performs an educational evaluation. Therefore, parents must be aware of the examiner's qualifications. At the very least, she should be a special educator with a master's degree in special education from an accredited university. (In some states the school psychologist administers these tests.) She should have experience administering a psychoeducational battery of tests. She should be familiar with LD children and experienced in evaluating children when there is a suspicion of a learning disability.

Beyond psychoeducational tests, information from parents about how their child does in school, what teachers report, how well he likes or dislikes school, how long it takes him to do homework, if he is easily distracted, and other descriptions of the child's behaviors will help to highlight the nature of the problem. A learning disability is a complex disorder, so the more information you can get from a wide variety of sources, the better able you are to thoroughly examine the critical areas.

With this in mind, it is a priority to get information from the child's teachers: classroom teacher, special subject teachers (music, art, physical education, computer), lunch-room monitor, playground monitors, and others who come into contact with the child in the school setting.

Once the evaluator has eliminated several areas of concern, she will use diagnostic tests in language, reading, writing, and math. These precise tests enable the evaluator to pinpoint strengths and weaknesses. She will also evaluate how the child processes information, examining his perceptual skills, memory skills, thinking skills, and attention skills.

Throughout this process the evaluator obtains specific scores on tests. These test scores are important, but equally important is the information the examiner gleans by watching the child as he works on the tests. (How does the child approach tasks, process information, stay on task, deal with frustration, and respond to reinforcement?) A child may score well on a math test but throw his pencil down when he can't figure out an answer. A child may pay more attention to the sound of the air conditioner than to the spelling test. A child may answer questions quickly, then change the answer after he has a while to think about it. These observations show the evaluator how the child functions in the academic setting.

Recently, there has been more emphasis placed on informal teacher-made tests and criterion-referenced tests—specifically curriculum based assessment (CBA). The student is evaluated based on his curriculum, not a standardized test that may be different from what he was taught. This allows the evaluator to more accurately measure progress in the curriculum and make comparisons with other students in the grade.

When this information is shared and discussed by other professionals, a clearer picture of the child's disorder begins to appear.

14

SOCIAL HISTORY

The purpose of the social history is to look at the home and the family situation in order to obtain information that will be useful in diagnosing learning disabilities. The social history should be taken by a licensed, certified social worker with an M.S.W. (master of social work) degree from an accredited university. (The criteria for certification varies from state to state.)

Like all members of a multidisciplinary team, the social worker should have experience with LD children and their families. At some time all members of the family are affected by the child with a learning disability. Information about the family and how they function may lead to effective interventions.

Parents and other family members may be asked to fill out a questionnaire or respond verbally to questions from a social worker. You may have been asked some of these same questions by the physician or psychologist. Each professional examines responses from his or her own professional perspective. The following information is typically sought in the social history questionnaires:

- Where do you live?
- Does anyone besides your immediate family live with you?
- Do you own your own home or do you rent?
- What is your occupation?
- How many years did you attend school?
- How is your health and that of other family members?
- Do you and your spouse have any marital problems?

- Length of pregnancy?
- Any problems with pregnancy or delivery?
- How does your child get along with siblings?
- Any history of school-related problems?
- Do both parents agree on child-rearing techniques?
- What kinds of parenting techniques work well with your child?
- Are you easily frustrated with your child's behavior?
- How do you deal with this frustration?

This information provides a sense of how the family functions. For example, if grandparents live with the family, do they help out with child care or are they ill and dependent on other family members? If you live in an apartment building, do you feel pressured to control your child's behavior because the neighbors complain? If you live in a rural area, do you feel there is no one you can go to for support? Where you live and who lives there will give the social worker insight into the most effective interventions for your family.

Both parents should respond to questions on the social history, even if they don't live in the same household. Unless a parent is totally absent from the child's everyday life, the information from both mother and father is important to the social worker's evaluation.

For a social history to be useful, it must be thorough. A quick checklist simply won't provide the multidisciplinary team with adequate information to make an accurate evaluation. And although some of the questions will have been asked by other members of the team, they will be viewed anew through the eyes of a social worker. Together, all members of the team will discuss their findings and provide parents with a complete picture of the child.

15

~~~~~~

SUMMARIZING RESULTS AND DRAWING CONCLUSIONS

Information from members of the evaluation team, class-room teachers, and parents is gathered and a team decision is made regarding the presence or absence of a learning disability in a child. It is important to remember that specific reasons are given when a teacher or parent makes a referral. Even if the student is not eligible for classification as learning disabled (or any other classification) it does not mean that she doesn't need some type of intervention. It simply means the intervention does not fall within the responsibilities of special education personnel.

Three major areas are considered before diagnosing learning disabilities: (1) intellectual functioning, (2) discrepancy between potential and performance, and (3) exclusionary clause.

Intellectual Functioning

Children with learning disabilities are often of average or above average intelligence. One way to ascertain intellectual functioning is by administering an intelligence test. When students are referred due to a suspected learning disability, an individually administered I.Q. test is given. The average I.Q. score is between 90 and 110. Therefore, in order to be classified as learning disabled the I.Q. score must be at least 90. It can be above the average range, but theoretically it should not fall below 90. The I.Q. cutoff for mental retardation is usually 70 (other criteria must also be met).

What to do with students who fall in the 71–89 range has become a considerable problem. In some cases the psychological report indicates that the lower I.Q. score does not represent true functioning. In other cases there is no discrepancy between the I.Q. score and school performance. And in still other cases it is noted that the student engages in behavior that reflects "average intellectual functioning."

Some have argued that the overreliance on average I.Q. scores eliminates students who are truly learning disabled, while others argue that it has led to the proliferation of students classified as learning disabled. Because of this controversy many states have included students with I.Q. scores between 75 and 90 as eligible for learning disabled services. If the I.Q. score is 70 or below, the child is not eligible for classification as learning disabled in most states.

Once the intellectual functioning level has been agreed on, the next step is to decide if a discrepancy exists between this level and academic performance.

Discrepancy Between Potential and Performance

Members of the multidisciplinary team examine the results of tests of academic ability and school performance. If there is a discrepancy between a student's potential and how the student performs in school, a learning disability may exist. For example, suppose a fourth grader has an average I.Q. score of 100. It would be expected that he would perform on the fourth grade level in standardized tests and his class grades would be average. If, however, he performs much lower than average and his test results are on the second grade level, there is reason for concern.

There was a great deal of discussion when Public Law 94-142 was being written as to how severe this discrepancy should be. As a rule, a "severe discrepancy" is viewed as 50 percent between performance and potential. Not all school districts follow this rule, and there are major problems associated with discrepancy formulas. However, as a guideline it suggests that not everybody who is slightly below grade level has a learning disability. Also, a discrepancy does not always indicate a learning disability. It may be due to other reasons that will be discussed in this key.

Exclusionary Clause

The last sentence of the definition of specific learning disabilities states:

> ". . . The term does not include children who have learning problems which are primarily the result of visual, hearing or motor handicaps, or mental retardation, of emotional disturbance, or of environmental, cultural, or economic disadvantage."

This has become known as the *exclusionary clause*. As the team meets to discuss the possibility of a learning disability they must rule out other reasons why the child is having difficulty in school.

This clause has caused considerable debate within the professional community. Questions have come up about whether a learning disability can coexist with other disabilities such as hearing or visual impairments. How can the primary disability be determined? Other issues beyond the scope of this book have been raised regarding the clause. In any case, the team must be able to conclude that the school problem is due to a learning disability, and is not the result of other difficulties cited.

Another concern to do with insuring that students receive appropriate interventions. If most everyone that has difficulty in school is classified as learning disabled, those who truly are learning disabled may not receive appropriate treatment. Also, for those students who have additional needs, or in the case of emotional disturbance, the classification of learning disabled is misleading, and they too may not receive appropriate treatment.

Finally, the need to find a label for every problem may be preventing those students who don't neatly fit into a category from receiving treatment they need. Some parents and teachers have referred children because they suspected a learning disability only to have the team decide the students were not learning disabled and did not meet the criteria for specific services. No suggestions for behavioral, emotional, or academic support were made, and the students and parents were left feeling helpless. Not every student who needs some type of assistance needs to receive it through the special education system, yet the school cannot just let them "fall through the cracks."

Pulling It All Together

The classic case of an average I.Q. score, a severe discrepancy between a child's potential and her performance in school, and no other reasons to explain such a discrepancy would together lead to the conclusion that the child should be classified as learning disabled. But not all cases are clear cut. Many students who are not learning disabled are classified as such for lack of another classification. They may have lower intellectual ability or emotional problems and the learning disabled label is used because it is perceived as less severe than other categories. In some cases it is difficult to document these other problems and in order to provide serious treatment, the LD label is employed.

Diagnostic decisions are not carved in stone. They represent a sample of how your child achieved under difficult circumstances. The results of any evaluation should only be thought of as a hypothesis or an educated guess. Success or failure over time in the school, home, and community will either affirm or reject that hypothesis.

Part Three

~~~~~~

THE EDUCATION
OF A CHILD WITH
A LEARNING
DISABILITY

Parents and schools must work cooperatively if children are to succeed. This is even more critical for children with learning disabilities. Children benefit when parents work with their schools and actively support them. In order to work in a collaborative manner parents need to be informed. This key addresses important issues and concerns regarding the education of a child with a learning disability. Some issues relate to services in the schools, others suggest things you can do at home. All the advice is intended to help parents and schools work together.

16

~~~~~~

IEP—
INDIVIDUALIZED
EDUCATION
PROGRAM

E very child who is classified as learning disabled must receive an IEP (Individualized Education Program). The National Information Center for Children and Youth with Disabilities (NICHCY) developed a fact sheet on frequently asked questions about an IEP:

What is an Individualized Education Program (IEP)?

An Individualized Education Program (IEP) is a written statement of the educational program designed to meet your child's special needs. The program should include statements of your child's strengths as well as weaknesses and should describe the instructional program developed specifically for your child. The IEP has two purposes: 1) to establish the learning goals for your child; and 2) to state the services that the school district is required to provide. The law requires that every child receiving special education services have an IEP, and that the child's parents have a right to receive their own copy of this document. It is important that you keep a copy of your child's IEP in order to check on your child's progress.

Who Develops My Child's IEP?

According to the law, the participants present at the IEP meeting should include the following:

- your child's teacher(s). (If your child has more than one teacher, your state may specify in its law which teacher should participate);
- a representative of the public agency other than your child's teacher;
- you, the parents—one or both;
- your child, when appropriate; and
- other individuals, at your discretion or at the discretion of your child's school.

What is Included in an IEP?

According to the law, an IEP must include the following statements regarding your child:

- his present level of educational performance, which could include comments on academic achievement, social adaption, prevocational and vocational skills, sensory and motor skills, self-help skills, speech and language skills, a transition plan (for those students age 14-1/2 or older) based on an evaluation and proper documentation;
- specific special education and related services to be provided and who will provide them;
- projected dates for the initiation and duration of special services;
- percentage of the school day in which your child will participate in regular education programs;
- short-term instructional objectives (individual steps that make up the goals);
- annual goals; and
- appropriate objective criteria and evaluation procedures to be used to measure your child's progress toward these goals on at least an annual basis.

Is it the School's Responsibility to Ensure that My Child Reaches all the Goals in His IEP?

No. The IEP is a guideline for individualized instruction, not a contract. The school is responsible only for providing the nstructional services described in an IEP.

What Occurs During an IEP Meeting?

The IEP meeting is scheduled for the purpose of developing a student's IEP. It is usually held at the child's school. The meeting takes place after the specialists have tested your child and recorded the test results. Your child's assessment results are usually explained at the IEP meeting. The specialists will explain what they did, why they used the tests they administered, the results of your child's tests, and what your child's scores mean when compared to other children of the same age and in the same grade. When possible, ask for the test results prior to the IEP meeting so that you can review and analyze them.

During the IEP meeting, you will be asked to share with the school the special things that you know about your child, including how your child behaves and gets along with others outside of school. You will be asked to present an overview of your child's school experiences and personal life. Everyone involved will then have a better idea of your child's needs.

If, on the basis of the information discussed in the meeting and the results of the assessment, it is decided that your child is eligible for special education or related services, an IEP must be developed. As a parent, you should understand why the school proposes the intervention it does. Before you sign the IEP, ask questions until you are sure that you understand what is being stated. You may request a review or revision of the IEP at any time.

If you cannot come to the IEP meeting, school personnel are to maintain records showing how they tried to find a time and place convenient for you. If neither parent can come to the meeting, the school must keep you informed by telephone or by mail of the meeting's outcome.

Federal law provides for the changing needs and growth of children. At least once a year, whether you request it or not, a meeting must be scheduled with you to review your child's progress and to develop your child's next IEP. A full re-evaluation must occur every three years. A re-evaluation may occur more often if you or your child's teachers request it; however, it cannot be scheduled more than once a year.

What Should I Do Before an IEP Meeting?

You can prepare for your child's IEP meeting by looking realistically at your child's strengths and weaknesses, visiting your child's class, and talking to your child about his feelings about school. It is a good idea to write down your ideas regarding what you think your child will be able to accomplish during the school year. Also, make notes about what you want to contribute during the meeting.

What Should I Do During the IEP Meeting?

As a parent, you are an important member of your child's IEP team. Listen carefully to the results of the tests, and make sure you understand what the tests are meant to measure and how the performance of your child compares to other children of the same age. Share with the team members any special information about your child, how he feels about school and how he gets along with family members. If you hear something about your child that surprises you or is different from the way you perceive your child, bring this to the attention of the other team members. In addition to sharing your feelings about your child's educational needs, consult with the other members of the team to design the best possible program for your child.

17

~~~~~~

EDUCATIONAL PLACEMENTS

Most students who are learning disabled are educated in regular classroom settings and receive special education services in a resource room during part of their school day.

Special education students are allowed ample time in the regular classroom. Although most states have guidelines for the amount of time to be spent in the resource room, the important factor is not the time allotment, but rather the fact that resource room placement is significantly different from placement in a special education self-contained classroom.

Students placed in a special education self-contained classroom spend most of the instructional day in this setting and receives their primary instruction from a special education teacher. In contrast, students placed in a resource room spend no more than half of the day in the resource room and receive only supplemental instruction from a special education teacher. Their primary instruction takes place in the regular classroom setting. The resource room teacher provides the student with the ways and means to succeed in the regular classroom. This arrangement represents a very different way of providing services to students with special educational needs.

Types of Resource Rooms

Three types of resource room programs are used in special education: (1) categorical; (2) cross-categorical (or multicategorical); (3) noncategorical

Categorical Resource Room Programs

Categorical resource rooms are those in which special education students are placed on the basis of their specific classification: learning disability, mental retardation, emotional disturbance. A school district using this type of program may have a number of resource rooms in operation, each room serving students with specific disabilities. There might be a resource room on the middle school level for students with learning disabilities, one for students who are emotionally disturbed (or behavior disordered), and still another for those students who are classified as educable mentally retarded.

The rationale for such an approach is that there are distinct, nonoverlapping special education categories, and the students within each of these categories have more in common with each other than they do with other students.

Cross-Categorical Resource Room Programs

In cross-categorical (or multicategorical) resource room programs students are placed on the basis of their specific needs rather than their particular classification. It would not be unusual in this type of arrangement to have students who are classified as learning disabled, mentally retarded, or emotionally disturbed placed in the same resource room.

Academic, social, physical, and behavioral needs must also be considered for effective programming. These variables can sometimes mean that students whose classifications are different have special needs that are very much alike. For example, most students with "mild disabilities" benefit from a structured classroom and perform better when tasks are broken into small components. A school district employing this type of program may have a resource room on the intermediate level with students who are classified as learning disabled, mentally retarded, and emotionally disturbed, but whose educational and emotional needs are somewhat similar. They may be reading on the same level, have similar language disorders, and low self-esteem. Most resource rooms are this type.

Noncategorical Resource Room Programs

This type of program may not be viewed strictly as a special education resource room program. The students are not classified in any of the special education categories. However, there are states and local school districts that employ this type of program using a certified special education teacher. The rationale is quite simple: There are students who need assistance but who may not be eligible for special education services. These "at-risk" students often receive resource room services as a trial to see if they need to be classified in order to receive additional special education services.

Certain school districts have great financial resources and provide these services without classifying students (and without receiving federal and state reimbursements). This approach is viewed as somewhat altruistic. While there are certain aspects of classification that may benefit students and their parents, advocates of noncategorical programs believe the negative aspects of labeling outweigh any benefits.

18

SUPPORT SERVICES

T his key focuses on a group of people who play a critical role in schools. Depending upon the terminology used by your school, they may be referred to as support services, ancillary services, child study teams, or building level teams. They represent a wide variety of services that are provided to students as they progress through the school years.

This key gives a brief description of various professionals in this group who provide much needed services. While licensing varies from state to state, most of these positions require a graduate degree (either a master's or doctorate depending on the state) and considerable supervision experience prior to working in a school setting. The work of some of these individuals may overlap, and at times they may take on different or additional responsibilities.

School Psychologist

The major responsibility of most school psychologists is to assess the intellectual and social-emotional status of students. They are frequently called upon to administer individual intelligence tests when there is a question of a student's ability to perform in school, and to evaluate a student's social-emotional status when this becomes a concern of parents and school personnel. In addition to these responsibilities, school psychologists may meet with individuals or groups of students to discuss psychosocial issues, consult with teachers regarding the most effective way to deal with specific students, and talk to parents regarding their child's school-related behavior. If a student encounters a problem that is beyond the scope of the school's assistance, the school psychologist can refer parents to outside sources.

School Social Worker

The responsibilities of the school social worker may include providing services to students and staff, such as: referrals to outside mental health facilities and public welfare agencies; information on substance abuse, alcoholism, and child abuse; and meeting with parent groups. School social workers may also function in a more therapeutic manner by counseling individuals or groups on a variety of issues, including: separation, divorce, depression, peer pressure, and suicide. When the needs of the student and her family cannot be accommodated in a school setting, the social worker can refer them to an appropriate outside agency.

Guidance Counselor

The majority of guidance counselors are employed on the secondary level (middle/junior/high school). Typically, they are responsible for assisting students with the selection of classes, career counseling, and post-secondary placements (college or vocational placement and employment). However, they may engage in other activities depending upon the grade placement and their own expertise. They may assist groups of students who are not working up to their potential, or smooth the transition between middle/junior high school and high school. Guidance counselors facilitate student teacher communication, especially when special education students are mainstreamed into regular classes. They also make appropriate referrals when a problem is beyond their expertise.

Remedial Reading Teacher

Most students learn to read with little or no difficulty. However, a small number of students encounter considerable trouble with this task. The services provided by the remedial reading teacher can be invaluable to these students.

Students are usually referred to this specialist by their classroom teacher when it is apparent that reading skills are not progressing at an appropriate rate. The remedial reading teacher will then administers individual or small group diagnostic reading tests that enable her to determine the current level of performance, the student's strengths and weaknesses, and information that will be useful in selecting the best reading approach. If the problem appears to be more than just reading, an appropriate referral can be made.

Most instruction is provided in small group or individual sessions, and the regular classroom teacher is consulted. Remedial reading teachers also work directly with other teachers to improve reading instruction on a school-wide basis.

Speech and Language Pathologist

When a child's speech or language is below the level expected for his age, he is often referred to the speech and language pathologist. A thorough assessment of speech and language functions are undertaken and an appropriate intervention plan is developed. Many parents think these specialists focuses primarily on speech problems such as articulation, voice disorders, and dysfluent speech. However, this represents only a small part of their responsibility. They spend considerable time working with students who have difficulty understanding language and being able to express their thoughts through language, both oral and written. They can also refer students to appropriate personnel if the problem encountered is greater than a speech/language impairment.

Other Related Services

Other support services include occupational therapy, physical therapy, music therapy, art therapy, dance therapy, and adaptive physical education. Although these services are provided infrequently, they are an integral component of a comprehensive support services program. Some of the students, but not all, who receive these services are in special education programs. In some school districts these services are provided by outside agencies on a confidential basis, and in other districts these programs are shared district-wide.

Parents should take advantage of the many support services available through their schools. By doing so, they will be able to make important decisions for their children and make their school years more productive and satisfying.

19

MAINSTREAMING

Mainstreaming is the placement of disabled students in regular classes with nondisabled peers. In many schools mainstreaming is the norm. Students with various intellectual, behavioral, learning, or physical disabilities, and attention deficits are placed in classes with their nondisabled peers.

Similarly, most students with learning disabilities are educated in the regular classroom, while receiving support services. The concept of Least Restrictive Environment (L.R.E.) is important in providing the most appropriate education placement for all students with special needs. This key examines the major issues in mainstreaming children with learning disabilities.

Concerns of Parents

Some parents are concerned that their children's needs will not be met in a regular classroom setting. However, mainstreaming does not mean that special education students are "dumped" into classes in an indiscriminate manner. Rather, care is taken so that students placed in a regular classroom can perform adequately, with support services. For example, a student may be in a regular second grade classroom and go to the resource room for help with reading. Or perhaps she is placed in a music class because of interest or ability in music. The music teacher and the special education teacher can discuss the student's progress.

The concept of mainstreaming includes the fact that students can benefit from regular classroom placement but must be provided with additional assistance, such as modification of instruction, additional time, or an aide. And that assistance includes communication with the regular classroom teacher.

Parents are also concerned that their child may be "picked on" in the regular classroom and be teased by his classmates. If this does occur, it can be easily rectified by a concerned and caring staff. Both students and staff must review training on the nature and needs of disabled children and adolescents so that they are treated like everyone else.

Parents of nondisabled children often complain that the disabled child might disrupt the class or take up a disproportionate amount of the teacher's time. Both are legitimate concerns. If a child, disabled or nondisabled, is so disruptive as to interfere with the functioning of the class, then intervention is necessary. Experience indicates that such children are not frequently mainstreamed; if they are mainstreamed, a well-controlled behavioral program is in place. Numerous disruptions occur in any classroom, and they are just as often caused by nondisabled children as disabled ones.

Concern about the teacher's time is often voiced. It is important to recognize that the regular classroom teacher should receive assistance when disabled students are mainstreamed into his class. That assistance may take the form of teacher consultation on specific methods and materials, demonstration lessons, or a teacher's aide in the classroom.

Regular classroom teachers often remark that the techniques they use for mainstreamed students are effective for all of their students. Some also say that the student with learning disabilities often takes up *less* of their time than other, more demanding students, who are not classified as special education students.

Making Mainstreaming a Success

Considerable time, energy, and planning go into every successful mainstreaming experience. Parents must be advocates for their children and provide input into the type and amount of mainstreaming that takes place. Most importantly, they need to forge positive relationships with school personnel. This should be done during the development and implementation of the IEP (Individualized Education Program).

Mainstreaming works when the following procedures are put into action:

- Parents and schools work cooperatively.
- Specific mainstreaming experiences are written on the child's IEP.
- Special education teachers meet with the teachers in the mainstreamed setting.
- Mainstreamed teachers receive information on the special education student's strengths, needs, and effective techniques.
- Mainstreamed teachers are provided with time to consult with the special education teachers to discuss student performance and progress.
- Regular classroom students are provided with information in order for them to better understand students with special needs.

Together, professionals and parents can make the mainstreaming experience a successful one for everyone concerned—teachers and students, disabled and nondisabled.

20

~~~~~~

INCLUSION

Inclusion—educating all children in regular classes regardless of disability—is a topic of heated discussion in special education circles, but for students with learning disabilities it does not represent a major change in the way they have been receiving special education services. The advocacy board of the Center on Human Policy at Syracuse University has the following statement on inclusion:

Inclusion Means:

1. Educating all children with disabilities in regular classrooms regardless of the nature of their disabling condition(s).
2. Providing all students with enhanced opportunities to learn from each other's contributions.
3. Providing necessary services within the regular schools.
4. Supporting regular teachers and administrators (e.g., by providing time, training, teamwork, resources, and strategies).
5. Having students with disabilities follow the same schedules as nondisabled students.
6. Involving students with disabilities in age appropriate academic classes and extracurricular activities, including art, music, gym, field trips, assemblies, and graduation exercises.
7. Allowing students with disabilities to use the school cafeteria, library, playground, and other facilities along with nondisabled students.

8. Encouraging friendships between nondisabled and disabled students.
9. Allowing students with disabilities to receive their education and job training in regular community environments when appropriate.
10. Teaching all children to understand and accept human differences.
11. Placing children with disabilities in the same schools they would attend if they did not have disabilities.
12. Taking parents' concerns seriously.
13. Providing an appropriate individualized educational program.

Inclusion Does Not Mean:

1. It does not mean dumping students with disabilities into regular programs without preparation or support.
2. It does not mean providing special services in separate or isolated places.
3. It does not mean ignoring children's individual needs.
4. It does not mean jeopardizing students' safety or well being.
5. It does not mean placing unreasonable demands on teachers or administrators.
6. It does not mean ignoring parents' concerns.
7. It does not mean isolating students with disabilities in regular schools.
8. It does not mean placing students with disabilities in schools or classes that are not age appropriate.
9. It does not mean requiring that students be "ready" and earn their way into regular classrooms based on cognitive or social skills.

Much more research needs to be undertaken before inclusionary placements for learning disabled students can be deemed more effective than other special education settings. This issue will continue to be a topic of debate among special education professionals and parents alike.

In January 1993 the Learning Disabilities Association of America issued a Position Paper on inclusion. It is presented here below.

The Learning Disabilities Association of America, LDA, is a national not-for-profit organization of parents, professionals, and persons with learning disabilities concerned about the welfare of individuals with learning disabilities. During the 1990-91 school year, 2,117,087 children in public schools in the United States were identified as having learning disabilities. This is more than 50 percent of the total number of students identified in all disability categories.

"Full inclusion," "full integration," "unified system," "inclusive education" are terms used to describe a popular policy/practice in which all students with disabilities, regardless of the nature or the severity of the disability and need for related services, receive their total education in their home school.

The Learning Disabilities Association of America does not support "full inclusion" or any policies that mandate the same placement, instruction, or treatment for **ALL** students with learning disabilities. Many students with learning disabilities benefit from being served in the regular education classroom. However, the regular education classroom is not the appropriate placement for a number of students with learning disabilities who may need alternative instructional environments, teaching strategies, and/or materials that cannot or will not be provided within the context of a regular classroom placement.

LDA believes that decisions regarding educational placement of students with disabilities must be based on the needs

71

of each individual student rather than administrative convenience or budgetary considerations and must be the result of a cooperative effort involving the educators, parents, and the student when appropriate.

LDA strongly supports the Individuals with Disabilities Education Act (IDEA) which mandates:

- a free and appropriate public education in the least restrictive environment appropriate for the students' specific learning needs.
- a team approved Individualized Education Program (IEP) that includes current functioning levels, instructional goals and objectives, placement and services decisions, and procedures for evaluation of program effectiveness.
- a placement decision must be made on an individual basis and considered only after the development of the IEP.
- a continuum of alternative placements to meet the needs of students with disabilities for special education and related services.
- a system for the continuing education of regular and special education and related services personnel to enable these personnel to meet the needs of children with disabilities.

LDA believes that the placement of **ALL** children with disabilities in the regular education classroom is as great a violation of IDEA as is the placement of **ALL** children in separate classrooms on the basis of their type of disability.

LDA URGES THE U.S. DEPARTMENT OF EDUCATION AND EACH STATE TO MOVE DELIBERATELY AND REFLECTIVELY IN SCHOOL RESTRUCTURING, USING THE INDIVIDUALS WITH DISABILITIES EDUCATION ACT AS A FOUNDATION—MINDFUL OF THE BEST INTERESTS OF ALL CHILDREN WITH DISABILITIES.

21

PARENTS' RIGHTS

Parents of children with learning disabilities have certain rights. These rights are presented in this key so parents can be aware of them. Most parent-school interactions are based on a desire to meet the needs of the child, not to do legal battle. However, parents should know exactly what they are entitled to by law, and in most cases, the school will inform them of this.

Your Right to Be Fully Informed and Your Right to Be Knowledgeable About the Actions to Be Taken

You must be fully informed of your rights, as well as adequately notified of proposed actions, their purpose, the intended results, decisions based on the actions, and the options considered in the educational decision-making process—all in your dominant language. You also have the right to examine and obtain copies of your child's school records.

Your Right to Participate

You have the opportunity to voice your opinion and participate in decisions through attendance at meetings and through your ongoing involvement in your child's education.

Your Right to Consent

You have the right to give or withhold consent in four situations:

- before the initial evaluation of your child;
- before placement of your child in special education for the first time;

- before starting your child in a 12-month special service or program;
- before a referral for adult services. A referral can be made when a student receiving nonresidential special education reaches age 15, and when a student receiving residential special education reaches age 18.

Your Right to File a Complaint

If you feel that one of the laws or regulations governing special education has been violated, you have the right to file a complaint. Your complaint needs to be in writing and should be directed to your state director of special education. The exact title varies in each state, so contact your state education department first.

It is important to note that you cannot initiate a complaint if your issue is unresolved at another level. For example, if a hearing has been initiated with an impartial hearing officer and no decision has been reached, you cannot file a complaint. If you do file a complaint, you will receive a written response indicating that your complaint will be investigated and resolved within 60 days. If there is evidence that a district has violated a law or regulation, compliance must be monitored until the underlying complaint is fully resolved.

Where the district has violated a law or regulation, the corrective action required must correct the problem not only for the particular child in question, but for all children. Once the investigation is complete, you will receive a written response. The letter must itemize each allegation and the findings on that allegation. A copy of this response will also be sent to the special education director and superintendent of the district. If you are not satisfied with the results of the investigation, an appeal may be submitted to:

Office of Special Education Programs
U.S. Department of Education
400 Maryland Avenue, S.W.
Washington, DC 20202

The OSE must keep copies of all correspondence. The correspondence logs of OSE must indicate the date of the response to you as well as the date of resolution.

Your Right to Independent Evaluation

If you disagree with the evaluation performed or obtained by the school district, you have the right to obtain an independent educational evaluation of your child. The district must pay for the independent evaluation, unless it initiates a hearing and the hearing officer determines that the district's evaluation is appropriate. If that happens, you may have an independent evaluation, but you must pay for it.

Your Right to Challenge

You have the right to request an impartial hearing to challenge decisions pertaining to your child's special education program. You have the right to bring an attorney or others knowledgeable about special education to represent you at the hearing. You are also entitled to receive a list of individuals and agencies that provide free or low cost legal services. You may also be able to receive reimbursement for attorney's fees incurred in special education disputes in which you prevail.

In some school districts, special education mediation is available at no cost. Mediation is a process in which you and a representative of the school district meet with an independent third party who assists in reaching agreement about issues or concerns regarding the recommendation of the committee on special education (CSE) or action of the board of education. In many cases, special education mediation has improved parent-school district communication and has resolved differences without the development of an adversarial relationship and with minimal emotional stress. To determine whether special education mediation is available in your school district, contact your school's CSE.

Your Right to Appeal

You have the right to appeal the decision of an impartial hearing officer to the state review officer and to seek judicial review of the state review officer's decision regarding your appeal.

22

∿∿∿∿∿∿∿∿∿∿∿∿∿∿∿∿∿∿∿∿∿∿∿∿∿∿∿∿∿∿∿∿∿∿∿

WHAT IS AN IMPARTIAL HEARING?

An impartial hearing is a formal procedure used to resolve disagreements between parents and school districts over the provision of special education.

You may choose formal due process procedures to challenge recommendations and decisions made by the school district. Similarly, in order to fulfill its responsibility to provide your child with a free, appropriate public education, the school district must initiate due process hearing procedures under certain circumstances. The impartial hearing has been established as a mechanism to hear both sides of the issues and fairly resolve the dispute through a third party.

When a request for an impartial hearing is made, the board of education must arrange a location for the hearing and appoint the hearing officer from the list of state certified hearing officers. Impartial hearing officers may not be employees of the district and may not have any personal professional interest that would conflict with their objectivity.

The impartial hearing is an administrative proceeding. Although it is somewhat like a court proceeding, the rules are relaxed. The hearing may be conducted in a session that is open or closed to the public. This decision is up to you.

The impartial hearing process includes:

- the calling of witnesses by both the school district and you to provide information and to respond to questions. The school district calls witnesses first, and you have the opportunity to ask questions of each witness. Then you have the opportunity to call witnesses, and the district can cross-examine;
- the prior exchange of documents to be used during the hearing by you and the school district, at least five days before the hearing;
- a written or electronic verbatim record of the proceedings, a copy of which must be made available to you;
- the provision of an interpreter for the deaf or a translator, if necessary; and
- the rendering of an impartial decision by the officer.

The hearing provides both parties with the opportunity to present their arguments to a hearing officer for a fair and legally correct resolution of the matter.

In order to assure impartiality, the hearing officer must tell both parties at the time of the hearing about any possible conflict of interest she may have. At that time, either party may object to that hearing officer being involved with the case any further and ask that she step down to allow the board of education to appoint another hearing officer.

Who is Involved at the Impartial Hearing?

Impartial Hearing Officer

The hearing officer must conduct a fair and impartial hearing and arrive at an independent decision based solely upon the evidence presented at the hearing. The hearing officer is appointed by the district from a list maintained by the board of education and certified by the state education department. Any person selected from the list must:

1) be independent and not be employed by the school district.
2) have no personal or professional interest that would interfere with his objectivity in the hearing.
3) not have participated in any manner in the formulation of the recommendations leading to the disagreement.
4) be certified by the commissioner as a hearing officer after taking an approved course and passing a test.

Parents

Parents are involved throughout the impartial hearing process unless they choose otherwise. You may request the hearing, prepare your case, and determine who attends the hearing. You decide whether the hearing is open or closed to the public.

Student

The student, in some instances, may attend the hearing to the extent deemed appropriate by you, the parent. An 18-year-old or emancipated minor may decide on her own to request an impartial hearing or to attend the hearing.

Representative for the School District

This person represents the board of education at the impartial hearing. This person may be the multidisciplinary chairperson or may be an attorney who arranges and presents the district's case at the hearing.

Representative for the Parents

Parents can also hire an attorney, advocate, or other representative, at their own expense, to assist them in organizing and participating in the hearing.

Guardian Ad Item

A hearing officer who feels that the interests of the parents are inconsistent with or are opposed to those of the child, or that the interests of the child would be best protected by someone else, may assign a guardian *ad item* for the child. In the event a guardian *ad item* is assigned, the hearing officer must assure that the parents' due process rights are preserved throughout the hearing.

Witnesses

Both parties may present witnesses to provide relevant information pertaining to their child's education and respond to questions regarding the disagreement over the provision of special education. Parents may ask the hearing officer to issue subpoenas to compel a witness to attend a hearing or to produce documents that they are unable to obtain voluntarily.

Stenographer

A stenographer may be employed to record the proceedings. If a stenographer is not used, the hearing must be tape-recorded to preserve the record, which is used to prepare a decision after the hearing. A verbatim record of the hearing must be made and be available to you and the school district.

Interpreter

The hearing officer will ask both parties about the need for an interpreter and make the necessary arrangements to have an interpreter of the deaf or of the dominant language of the child's home present at the hearing.

When is an Impartial Hearing Requested?

Requests for Impartial Hearings by Parents

You may request an impartial hearing to challenge any determination regarding your child's right to a free, appropriate public education. A request for a hearing should be made after the multidisciplinary team and the board of education have rendered their decision.

Requests are made after informal methods to resolve the issue have been exhausted. A request for an impartial hearing must be made in writing and should be made as soon as you decide that your child's needs are not being met and the problems cannot be informally resolved. Some reasons for requesting for a hearing are

- disagreement with the recommendation
- failure by the multidisciplinary team to evaluate a child and make its recommendation within 30 school days of consent
- failure to implement the multidisciplinary team's recommendation within 30 school days
- failure of the board of education to review, at least annually, the child's program, or failure to reevaluate the child every three years
- disagreement with the special education provided.

Impartial Hearings Initiated by the School District

The board of education is responsible for ensuring that a student with a disability receives a free, appropriate public education. To fulfill its responsibilities in this process, the board of education must initiate an impartial hearing when:

- You do not consent to the initial evaluation and the referral has not been withdrawn by mutual agreement. In those cases, the board of education must initiate an impartial hearing to obtain permission to conduct an evaluation despite the absence of parental consent to the evaluation.
- The school district wants to establish that its evaluation is appropriate to avoid paying for an independent evaluation.
- You withdraw consent to an evaluation or to a proposed placement.

23

KEEPING THE RECORD STRAIGHT

Parents' File

What to keep? What to discard? It is not easy to decide what or how much of your children's school materials to keep. You can hardly discard that wonderful essay on "What Thanksgiving Means to Me" or those precious mementos of the first times they wrote their names.

It is probably a good idea to keep two separate files (or piles) of information. Old workbooks, essays, and such provide wonderful memories for both parents and children. One file can contain these old papers and projects.

One file, however, should be kept in a more organized and sequential fashion. A simple manilla folder or large envelope will do for each school year and each child. In it place report cards, all parent teacher correspondence, and a few samples of work. Three or four samples of school work in each subject area can be selected from different periods of the school year.

Easy access to this information is critical when you have to make educational decisions. For example, a child is placed in a particular reading group, solely on the basis of standardized test scores. Her parents feel that their daughter's classroom performance—based on report cards, teacher comments, and work samples—indicates she could perform at a higher level. By providing the school with this information in a timely fashion, the girl's parents can provide constructive input into the school's decision-making process.

These records are even more important when there is a suspicion of a learning disability. Your file will provide a chronology of events and will facilitate the referral, identification, and classification process.

The burden of record-keeping is not entirely on the parents; however, it is wise for parents to proceed as if it were.

School's Records

Each state has laws regarding how long records must be kept. Immunization, attendance, and special education records are just a few types that are governed by specific state and federal guidelines. In order to find out exactly what the requirements are in your district, call your superintendent's office.

Most parents are concerned about the records that are kept on file in their children's school. You are entitled to examine these records. Typically, you will find standardized test scores, report cards, and teacher correspondence. Due to the fact that these are open files and parents have access to them, rarely will you find much besides the standard information collected on students. If you examine the file and find information you think is inappropriate ask the school's principal for the procedures to follow in order to have this information expunged.

Special legislation governs record-keeping procedures for children with learning disabilities. Upon graduation, or a student's reaching age 21, the only records that can be sent to other schools, agencies, or potential employers are the name of the student, address, years of attendance, and courses taken. No mention of the disability or any other confidential information can be supplied.

Finally, in some cases in which a student is seeing a psychologist, social worker, or drug and alcohol counselor, the information is kept entirely confidential, even from the child's parents. Check with your local school board or state department of education to ascertain specific guidelines regarding these files.

The "Well-Filed" Parent

Easily accessible school and personal records come in handy when information is needed to help make educational decisions for your children. Review your home files periodically; keep what you need or want and discard the rest. Also, examine the school's files regularly.

The time and effort you put into organizing this information will be well spent if you are called to make a decision affecting your child's education, or if you question a decision made by the school. Moreover, the information you collect will be a wonderful source of memories for you and your children.

24

~~~~~~

COLLEGE

The first college program for students with learning disabilities was established in 1970 at Curry College in Milton, Massachusetts. Since then there has been a rapid increase in such programs, which now number over 1,000. These programs are a logical progression as students with learning disabilities move beyond high school. Not all students with learning disabilities have the capability or initiative to pursue a college degree, but for many students these programs mean the difference between success and failure during the college years.

If you are interested in such a program, consult your child's guidance counselor early in this junior year, or if the guidance counselor is unaware of such programs, consult one of these guides:

Peterson's Guide to Colleges with Programs for Learning Disabled Students (Published every year.)

Peterson's Guides
Princeton, NJ

or

A Guide to Colleges for Learning Disabled Students

Academic Press, Inc.
Orlando, Florida 32887

These guides provide current information on the colleges as well as specific information about the L.D. programs, such as availability of services, student-teacher ratio, available assistance, counseling services, and contact people. This is all very important because the programs vary greatly. For example, some programs use peer-tutors (other college students) and pay them an hourly wage, whereas others have full-time faculty with expertise in the area of learning disabilities.

The criteria for admission vary as much as they do for any college. Generally, two-year programs have an open admission policy. Four-year colleges may also have this policy, but more often they have a selective admission policy.

Students must provide the college with documentation that they have a learning disability. Usually this is an IEP, but schools may require other kinds of information. In order to insure that the student is capable of college-level work an individual test of intellectual ability is usually requested. Also, in addition to an interview with the student, the school may request an interview with the parents.

Students with learning disabilities are eligible for testing modification on the Scholastic Achievement Test (SAT) or the American College Testing Program Assessment (ACT). Speak to your guidance counselor for the specific requirements and the addresses of these organizations.

College programs for students with learning disabilities typically provide diagnostic testing, advisement, counseling, remediation, tutoring, special courses, and auxiliary aids and services. Some of the aids and services cited in the *Peterson's Guide* are explained here.

Auxiliary Aids and Services

Colleges with programs for learning disabled students offer a number of auxiliary aids and services to help them compensate for their disabilities. Auxiliary aids include tape recorders, taped textbooks, calculators, typewriters, and word processors. Auxiliary services include the assignment of note-takers, alternative arrangements for taking course examinations, advocacy, and special housing arrangements.

Tape Recorders and Taped Textbooks

Learning disabled students often have difficulty taking notes on class lectures. The tape recorder becomes a valuable auxiliary aid for these students. They are able to tape-record a lecture while they take notes. Later, they can replay the tapes to check their notes for completeness and accuracy. The use of a tape recorder reduces the demands upon learning disabled students' auditory memory, language processing, and writing skills. Professors are encouraged to allow learning disabled students to use tape recorders in their classes.

Taped textbooks are used by learning disabled students who have difficulty reading college-level materials. College learning disabilities program staff members help such students to obtain taped textbooks from Recording for the Blind and from the Library of Congress's National Library Service for the Blind and Physically Handicapped.

These staff members familiarize students with the services of Recording for the Blind and the Library of Congress and help them complete the necessary application forms. They also help students determine the textbooks needed for future courses to enable the students to submit applications for taped textbooks in sufficient time to receive books prior to the beginning of a new term.

Calculators, Typewriters, and Word Processors

Calculators, typewriters, and word processors are additional aids provided by some college learning disabilities programs. Calculators are used by students who have not mastered computational skills to an automatic level. Typewriters are made available to learning disabled students who have poorly developed handwriting skills that interfere with their ability to produce written assignments. Word processors assist in writing term papers. Students are able to store what they write and make whatever revisions are necessary. A word-check program may be used to identify and correct misspelled words.

Note-takers

Note-takers are non-learning disabled students who attend the same classes with the learning disabled students. They have been identified as good note-takers who are reliable, competent in the subject, and have legible handwriting. A duplicate set of notes is given to the learning disabled student through an intermediary member of the learning disabilities program staff. Usually, the note-taker does not know the identity of the student receiving the notes.

Alternative Examination Arrangements

Alternative arrangements are provided for students who have difficulty taking examinations in the usual manner. Often learning disabled students have difficulty completing a test within a specified time limit, accurately reading test questions, and writing answers. Staff members from the learning disabilities program make arrangements with professors to allow students to take course examinations with one of a number of alternatives:

- Extended time limits
- Questions dictated onto an audiotape
- Questions read by a proctor
- Responses dictated onto audio tapes
- Responses dictated to a proctor
- Questions presented in a different format (e.g., multiple choice in place of essay)

- Take-home examinations or projects in place of written examinations

Advocacy

Members of college learning disabilities staffs also serve as advocates for learning disabled college students. They work with professors to ensure that students are given every legitimate opportunity to succeed in their courses. Some of the advocacy activities performed by program staff members include:

- requesting lists of required textbooks for taping
- obtaining permission for students to tape-record lectures
- obtaining permission to use a non-class member as a note-taker
- requesting opportunities for students to take tests in alternative ways
- arranging for incomplete grades when students need more time to complete a course
- arranging for withdrawal from a course without a grade penalty when extra time is not the solution
- helping professors understand the needs of learning disabled students
- making suggestions to professors for modifying their teaching style to enhance the learning opportunities for LD students

A goal of learning disabilities programs is to have students become their own advocates. Therefore, the activities and roles performed by program staff members are phased out as students develop increasing independence.

Housing

Careful consideration is given to housing arrangements for learning disabled students. Programs vary with respect to specific dormitory arrangements. In some, learning disabled students live together in special dormitories. In others, learning disabled students are assigned to dormitories with their non-learning disabled peers. In any case, program staff members ensure that such students have access to a quiet, nondistracting environment for study, and that they are adequately supervised.

Selecting Learning Disabilities College Programs

The following questions should be considered when looking at college programs

1. Are the following items used to evaluate learning disabled students for admission?

   - Untimed SAT or ACT
   - Letters of recommendation
   - Autobiographical statement
   - Psychoeducational report
   - Personal interview

2. Is diagnostic testing available to learning disabled students?
3. Is subject area tutoring available?
4. Is basic skills remediation available?
5. Do staff members of the learning disabilities program as well as academic advisers help learning-disabled students plan their academic program?
6. Are special courses available?
7. Are the following auxiliary aids provided?

   - Taped textbooks
   - Tape recorders
   - Calculators
   - Typewriters
   - Word processors
   - Other

8. Are the following auxiliary services provided?

   - Alternative exam arrangements

- Note-takers
- Advocacy
- Others

9. Are the following counseling services available?

- Individual
- Small-group
- Rap sessions
- Career
- Others

Many students with learning disabilities have successfully completed college and have gone on to productive careers—however, not without considerable work. Such students recognize that it takes hard work but feel that their efforts have yielded great results. The key for both parent and student is to start the preparation and selection process early to ensure a good match between the student's needs and the college program.

Part Four

~~~~~~

THE LEARNING DISABLED CHILD AT HOME

L earning disabilities don't disappear at 3 o'clock or on weekends. Every aspect of a child's life can be affected by this disability. Simple routines, such as meals, bedtimes, and homework, can cause problems in the home for the entire family. This part of the book gives gives parents information to help them deal effectively with their child at home.

25

MANIFESTATIONS AT HOME

It is not unusual for a parent of a child with a learning disability to lament, "she's so disorganized," or "he knocks everything over," or make other complaints about their child's behavior at home. Learning disabilities are not restricted to school. And yet because it is often thought of as a school-based disorder parents may not recognize the ways in which a learning disability may manifest itself at home. Let's take a typical day and see how a learning disability may interfere with everyday activities.

Getting Ready for School

For many people, morning is not the best time of day. You may be tired, feel rushed, and have the events of the day on your mind. Add to this a learning disability and it's no wonder that many parents of learning disabled children find the morning a difficult time. Some children dislike going to school and experiencing failure so much that they engage in behavior that will make them miss their bus or ride to school. Other students may underestimate the amount of time it takes for a specific activity, such as a shower, eating, or getting dressed, and cause considerable turmoil in the household.

Children who have difficulty with fine motor skills may take longer to get dressed and have problems with eating breakfast, not to mention the child with perceptual problems who frequently knocks over the milk. At times it may appear that your child is doing this on purpose. However, usually these are simply ways that the learning disabilities manifest themselves in behavior at home.

One way to resolve many problems in the morning is for the parent to wake up at least a half-hour earlier than usual in order to be ready to do what he must *before* the children get up. If you have to worry about being dressed it makes the situation more difficult.

Follow the same routine every day. Make sure all your children eat, get dressed, and are ready for school before watching TV or playing games. You may find using a kitchen timer helpful. Many parents wake up their children and set the timer for the amount of minutes they have to get dressed, brush teeth, wash, and so on, and only after these tasks are completed are they "rewarded" with TV or other leisure activities.

Parents who frequently praise their children for appropriate behavior find that is helpful, too. These procedures work for *all* children, not just children with learning disabilities. It is crucial that siblings understand the nature of their brother or sister's disability (see Appendix C), but they also must know that parents are fair and equitable.

After School

After school activities can also present problems for children with learning disabilities. Homework is usually the main issue for parents of children with learning disabilities. Many children forget what they have to do. It's a good idea to get a separate small assignment book just for homework. Also, if possible, have an extra set of books at home in case your child forgets them. Some parents purchase them, and some school districts provide them to children who have a hard time remembering.

After school homework time should be structured and supervised by an adult. Some children with learning disabilities need a great deal of help organizing their time, and this time of day is particularly troublesome.

Dinner Time

Traditionally, dinner time has been the best time of day to meet as a family and discuss the day's events. Today, too many parents say that this is an impossible time of the day due to busy schedules and interpersonal problems among family members; thus, the family does not eat together.

In every family, though, it's worth the effort to try and have a meal together and to ask children to pitch in. However, you should know how your child's learning disabilities may manifest themselves in chores like these. For example, if your child is responsible for setting the table and is always short a few utensils, you should understand it might be due to his inability to match object to number. The child who takes too much on her plate merely may not be able to estimate. Children who always seem to knock over things at the table may have an attention or perceptual deficit. Constant bickering may be due to social perceptual problems.

Once again structure is important. Assign tasks for each of your children and avoid those that may cause problems. Place spillable objects away from your child and encourage *everyone* to pass items around—not across—the table.

Sometimes it may be necessary to seek professional help to eliminate the tension and hostility that accompanies meals, but initially positive reinforcement may work.

Keeping Calm

Rather than verbally reprimanding or punishing behavior that you find annoying, first try to determine if it's a manifestation of the child's learning disability. A child who has difficulty zippering her jacket or tying her shoelaces because of fine motor problems will never learn how to do these tasks through

95

punishment. The task needs to be broken down into small steps and the child should be rewarded for completion of each step. You may find that zippering is too difficult and that you should avoid zippers as much as possible. At best you are recognizing that this is not a sign of defiance but rather a legitimate learning disability.

Speak to members of your multidisciplinary team and your child's teacher. Ask them for specific examples of how your child's learning disability may manifest itself at home. They should be able to provide you with examples—and solutions. Too many parents realize too late that a lot of the annoying things their children do are because of their learning disabilities, and the parents feel terrible for having punished them. Parents can eliminate this source of guilt by knowing when their children's actions are related to their learning disability.

26

~~~~~~

READING

M ost students with learning disabilities are referred because of a reading disorder. Because reading is a major area of concern for children with learning disabilities two keys in this book are devoted to it. This key is an overview of reading instruction in schools; the next key emphasizes things parents can do to help motivate their children to read.

Parents of children with learning disabilities should be aware of the reading approach that is used in their school. Many different reading programs are employed in schools throughout the United States, but they generally fall into one of the following seven approaches.

1. Visual Approaches

Visual methods are often referred to as "look-say" because words are taught by visual discrimination of letters and remembering what several letters grouped together look like. The contours of the words are highlighted in order to help children distinguish and remember them.

Many basal readers (graded series for the average reader) incorporate a visual approach in beginning reading. Eventually decoding skills are added. Comprehension is emphasized throughout.

2. The Phonics Approach

The phonics method teaches children to associate printed letters with their corresponding sounds. Children can then use these phonic skills to analyze sound sequences, blend them, and pronounce new words. For example *pond* may be sounded out (pu-ah-nn-di) and then blended again. A variety of reading series emphasize the phonics method.

3. The Linguistic Approach

Linguistic theorists emphasize the strong relationship between printed words and the reader's oral language. The linguistic approach combines visual and phonics methods. Word stems like *at* and *ick* are taught as sight words and individual sounds are substituted at the beginning of the stem: *pat, cat; sick, pick, kick.* Stems are taught that can be placed at the beginning (e.g., *un, dis*), end, or middle of words. There is a definite sequence to the presentation of words, regular spelling patterns first, followed by irregular forms, and so on.

4. Language Experience Methods

The language experience method emphasizes comprehension because the child's language is the foundation upon which reading skills are built. The child uses his vocabulary to orally relate personal experiences. The teacher writes these on wall charts. After the child can answer meaningful questions about his story, he is directed to look at the individual words and letters and try to remember them. Activities such as illustrating, editing, and making permanent charts or books are encouraged. This approach encourages creativity, motivation for learning to read, and aids speaking, listening, spelling, and writing skills.

5. Personalized Reading Approach

The personalized reading approach has been adopted by many alternative schools that wish children to read what is most meaningful to them. The goal is to erase the stigma (of being behind everyone else) that comes from being assigned to the "Blue Bird" reading group instead of the "Hawks." It represents a much broader way of thinking about reading than other approaches.

The student chooses material that is of personal interest (books, magazines, newspapers) and reads at his or her own pace. It is highly motivating for students to participate in this type of independent approach.

6. Programmed Instruction

Programmed instruction materials are the most extreme behavioral-oriented materials. They allow the student to be actively involved in learning and to progress at her own pace. The teacher is merely a guide. Programmed materials are presented in small sequential steps. The reader gets immediate feedback about whether or not her answers are correct, and then engages in additional examples of those skills in which she needs further practice.

7. Whole Language Approach

A whole language approach seeks to immerse students in a supportive, stimulating, natural learning environment that promotes their literacy. In a whole language approach, reading, writing, listening, speaking, and thinking are integrated as part of each lesson and activity.

In a whole language approach, the emphasis is on reading for meaning rather than learning decoding skills in isolation. Students are motivated to read and improve their reading by reading real, relevant and functional materials. Rather than using basal readers or skill development programs, whole language reading materials are fiction and nonfiction books and resources the students need or want to read. Thus, the whole language classroom is stocked with books of varying degrees of difficulty and content such as novels, short stories, dictionaries, and encyclopedias.

27

MOTIVATING YOUR
CHILD TO READ

Parents sometimes say they can't get their children away from the television or video game. They want them to do something productive, such as read a good book, yet their cries go unattended. Why is it that some children are more interested in reading than others? Two factors seem to affect this behavior the most: the parents' attempt to instill a love of literature in the child at an early age, and whether the parents are good role models (avid readers). For children with learning disabilities these factors are critical. They need to see that reading is more than just another academic skill.

Start Early

You can't force a child to read. What you must do is begin to develop the appreciation of books and reading at a very early age. Children usually love being read to. Select songs and nursery rhymes that stimulate a child. Show them picture books that are simple yet vivid, in order to capture their attention. The more you provide them with this type of stimulation, the more likely they are to view books as enjoyable.

Most children have bedtime rituals. This is an opportune time to read to them, to talk about large picture books, and to make them aware of the printed word. Initially, keep reading time brief, but as children get older or show increased interest, expand the time. Before you know it you may run out of books.

The selection of books is important. Some key considerations are as follows.

Selecting Books

Visit your local library. They have story hours and other activities designed to motivate children to read. Talk to the children's librarian for guidance about appropriate books and authors.

Look for a book store that treats children's books with the seriousness they deserve. Store personnel can greatly assist you in making selections. Many children's bookstores also have story hours, book fairs, or other free or low-cost activities that you and your children may find enjoyable.

A wealth of beautifully illustrated, well-written books are available for children. Don't restrict your choice because you think your children will not appreciate them. Teach them to respect and value good books. Also, consider the interests of your children and find an author that they each like. Foster interest in particular types of books and as they continue to read more frequently their reading will become more varied.

When in doubt over a selection, go with a book *you* enjoy. If you like the pictures, the story, or the message, your children will also probably enjoy it.

Developing Lifelong Habits

As your children become increasingly aware of the world around them, your own reading habits will greatly influence their behavior. Children need to see their parents reading on a regular basis and with a wide variety of reading materials. A home should be stocked with newspapers, magazines, and books in all rooms. The more you demonstrate the knowledge and joy to be accrued from reading, the more likely your children will emulate your behavior. Conversely, you can lecture and force your children to read all day long, but if they don't see you reading or if your home is devoid of ample reading material your demands will be ignored.

Don't try to teach your children to read. As the authors of *Raising Readers* suggest, "Forget about teaching the child to read. Just enjoy literature with them." The following books can help you get started.

Butler, D. *Babies Need Books*. NY: Atheneum, 1980.

Freeman, J. *Books Kids Will Sit Still For*. Hagerstown, MD: The Alleyside Press, 1984.

Hall McMullan, K. *How to Choose Good Books for Kids*. Reading Mass: Addison-Wesley, 1984.

Hearne, B. *Choosing Books for Children: A Commonsense Guide*. NY: Delacorte Press, 1981.

Lanne, L.L., Lox, V., Matengo, J., and Olson, M. *Raising Readers*. NY: Walker and Co., 1980.

Oppenheim, J., Brenner, B., and Boegehold, B.D. *Choosing Books for Kids* NY: Ballantine Books, 1986.

Trelease, J. *The Read-Aloud Handbook*. NY: Penguin Books, 1985.

Many of these books are broken down according to age or school grade. Most provide excellent bibliographies of children's books, and others list specific guidelines parents should follow (see Jim Trelease's excellent do's and don'ts for reading aloud).

28

MOTIVATING YOUR CHILD TO LEARN

A child's ability to perform well in school is affected by many factors, including how motivated he is to do so and his self-perception. A child who sees himself as a successful, enthusiastic learner is more apt to meet that expectation.

Parents must attempt to provide a home environment that is warm, positive, encouraging, and supportive. The type of home that values learning, builds successful experiences, praises positive efforts, and refrains from threats and damaging negative statements will instill enthusiasm for learning.

One way to instill positive learning and success is to give children tasks that are broken down into manageable components. This allows the child to experience a sense of accomplishment. Success becomes contagious; the more successful experiences children have, the more willing they become to take risks. As children begin to feel good about their performance, they tend to have higher expectations for success. Professional literature has clearly documented the relationship between this kind of expectation and performance.

Conversely, if most children's attempts at learning are met with failure, they will become discouraged. This is not to suggest that children will never meet with failure; however, parents can provide many experiences at home that will instill an internal belief of "I can do it" in their children.

Parents need to be aware that these early experiences can shape how children feel about learning. There should be a balance between providing meaningful, successful experiences and dealing with failure in a matter-of-fact manner.

Ways to Motivate an Unmotivated Child

You can't make your children enthusiastic about school or force them to learn when they are not so inclined. What you *can* do is provide your child with an atmosphere that instills a sense of enthusiasm and joy for school and provides support and reinforcement for their efforts.

Be a Positive Role Model

You can talk about a "love of learning" and the "importance of a good education," but if you do not demonstrate your commitment to these values, your children will see them as meaningless. Learning is a life-long task, not something confined to the school years. The more your children see your sense of enthusiasm, the more likely they are to follow your lead. Be willing to try new tasks and activities, demonstrate a positive attitude about your abilities, and attempt to learn new skills throughout your lifetime.

Be Supportive of Your Child's School

Let your child know that you value what the school does. Become an active member of the parent/teacher organization (PTA/PTO), or participate in school-wide activities. If you are not pleased with classroom procedures or school policies, for example, speak to the principal or teacher and express your feelings. School administrators are more receptive to criticism if they sense an atmosphere of mutual respect and cooperation between school and home. Do not frequently criticize the school system or your children's teachers in the presence of your children because this tends to undermine everyone's efforts.

Demonstrate that Learning Takes Place Everywhere

Visit museums, see plays and movies, and do other activities that all family members can enjoy, learn from, and discuss together. Activities or trips should be fun and different from those at school, and should emphasize learning in an unstructured, spontaneous or adventurous way.

Break Down Activities and Tasks into Small Components

Don't overwhelm your child with tasks that are too complex. Keep tasks simple and short at first, and gradually increase the task demands as your child's proficiency increases. The goal is to increase their rate of success, not to discourage them. Your verbal instructions should be clear and simple. For example, rather than tell your child to "get ready for school," you could break that task into the following steps:

1. Go to the bathroom
2. Wash
3. Get dressed
4. Sit at breakfast table
5. Eat breakfast
6. Brush teeth
7. Get school bag
8. Get lunch
9. Get coat
10. Get going!

Reinforce Appropriate Behavior

To reinforce appropriate behavior, praise your child's efforts and let him know that he is valued and appreciated. As children begin to feel good about their accomplishments, you still need to praise them but not necessarily for every effort. Children may need more reinforcement at some times than at others. If you reinforce them when they are good, the times

105

when they are not will diminish. Also, learn what kind of reinforcement is most effective.

Don't Criticize Your Children

For children with learning disabilities who are unmotivated and lack confidence, criticism merely reinforces their low self-esteem.

29

~~~~~~

MAKE LEARNING FUN

It's often been said that parents are their children's first teachers. Clearly, the interaction that occurs between a parent and a child sets the tone for learning. The parents' styles of presentation, their personalities, the experiences they provide, and the behaviors they model also form the foundation of learning.

It is critical that parents be good role models for their children. If parents want their children to feel good about reading, for example, then they must read; if they want them to be curious about the world around them, they must be equally curious; and if they want them to become avid learners, then it is imperative that they love learning.

Specifically, parents need to show enthusiasm when approaching new tasks or knowledge. They need to demonstrate that effort leads to results, and even when the desired results don't occur, learning always takes place. Both children and parents learn from failing. Adults need to take risks in learning; otherwise, they will limit not only their own opportunities, but those of their children.

Children who see parents approach tasks in a positive, thoughtful manner are likely to do the same. This positive attitude does not mean that both mom and dad will engage in the same task, or that when they do, they'll have the same learning style.

Activities Outside the Home

The more experiences that parents give their children, the more likely their language and literacy skills will be enhanced. Children don't require expensive vacations in order to build up their vocabulary. A variety of activities close to home can enhance learning.

One parent, for example, takes her child to the beach every weekend. During the week, she and the child checked out books from the local library about beaches and read them. The books covered many topics including wildlife, ecological issues, and types of fish.

When they go to the beach they discuss the books and take pictures of whatever interests them. Once the pictures are developed, they are placed on construction paper and the youngster dictates a few sentences about each picture. By the end of the summer, he has written his own book about the beach. All of this is accomplished in a pressure-free, low-structure environment that is both fun and very educational.

Other parents have done the same type of thing by helping their children explore different neighborhoods in large cities like New York, sampling ethnic foods, visiting specialty shops, and learning about different cultures. These parents demonstrated to their children that learning new information is enjoyable.

Most libraries have story hours or book discussions for children of various ages. Children's book stores frequently sponsor special guest authors and other activities related to reading. A local carnival, a baseball game—any experience—can serve as a springboard for learning.

In the Home

Finally, parents can do many things in their home to facilitate learning. The benefits of reading to children are widely known, but the point bears repeating. Parents should read to their children! Let them know the wonders of the written word!

All the rooms of the home should be stocked with books, magazines, and newspapers, and parents should discuss what they read with their children. They need to reinforce discussion instead of telling them to be quiet! When parents don't know the answer to a child's question, they should help the child find it. All quests for knowledge should be recognized and reinforced; otherwise, parents risk turning their children off to learning at an early age. It takes very little to let children know that their thirst for knowledge is appreciated, but it takes even less to quench it.

One way to facilitate learning in the home is to limit television viewing. When children watch too much television, they tend to act in a passive manner. Videos too often become babysitters. The same can be said for computer programs. Even if they are educational, electronic media cannot take the place of the learning that occurs during conversations and activities between children and adults.

This principle also applies to toy selection. Parents should not overload children with toys, particularly toys that "do everything." Toys that require very little thinking to use foster very little learning. The best toys require a child to use her imagination and creativity. Blocks, for example, can be whatever a child wants to build with them; whereas a toy fire truck can only be a fire truck.

30

ESTABLISHING SCHOOL ROUTINES

Setting home routines provides children with stability and a logical order of events that helps them to organize their day. You needn't always conform to rigid getting-ready-for-school, doing-homework, or going-to-bed schedules when logic dictates otherwise. For example, special events, family functions, or additional school activities may require a change in routine.

School Mornings

Getting ready for school can be a major source of stress in a family, especially if both parents have to be out of the house at the same time. One way to alleviate some early morning complaints is to select clothes for the morning prior to going to bed.

School bags (containing completed homework!), musical instruments, and other necessary items should also be readied and put in the same place every school night, perhaps on a table near the door so they are not forgotten. When you and your children listen to the weather forecast the night before school, you can also discuss the coat or jacket to be worn before the rush of the morning routine.

Aside from important nutritional benefits, eating a good breakfast helps establish a school routine and, if enough time is allowed, provides time to talk and prepare for the world of school. If your family finds that mornings are too chaotic for a calm breakfast, try rising an hour earlier than your children or otherwise adjusting the schedule to make time for it.

After School

The most important routine that is best established early in a child's school career is when and how homework is to be done. Create a comfortable routine so that you are not battling over the completion of homework well into the evening.

An increasing number of children come home to a babysitter who needs to follow the same routine that you have established for doing homework. If your children are home alone after school, you can establish a routine where they call you at a specific time each day and they follow a written schedule you post at home. Children should also have easy access to the name and phone number of a neighbor (who is usually at home) for emergencies, as well as a list of emergency phone numbers near the phone.

As mentioned, you need to be flexible in establishing routines to accommodate changes in your children's school schedules or extracurricular activities. Also, be careful not to over-schedule your children's time. They need your help in organizing their free time, but every minute need not be filled with a structured activity. Besides being stressful and leaving children no time to themselves or for spontaneous activities, over-scheduling can make it impossible for children to successfully meet the demands of their daily routines.

31

HOMEWORK

Many parents of children with learning disabilities dread homework. The primary purpose of homework is to reinforce a previously learned skill. Homework is not the way to introduce a new skill or practice skills that are not fully developed. Ideally, the teacher will teach a particular skill during class and then—but only after the student demonstrates mastering a skill—assign a few examples of using that skill for homework. This enables the student to practice the skill outside the classroom.

If homework is not assigned in this process, it can become the source of unnecessary battles between parents and children. For learning disabled children homework takes on even more importance. Children want to perform well for their parents, and parents are anxious about their children's performance. These two factors heighten the tension and anxiety that accompany an academic task for such a student. Some parents do remarkably well when helping their children with homework, but many do not. Even if you don't work directly with your child, the following suggestions may help the situation.

1. Children should have a place to do their homework that is relatively free of distractions. It should be the same place every day.
2. Homework should be done right after school. Of course, children must be allowed to relax after school—have a snack, talk about the day's events—

but they can begin their assignments within an hour or so.

3. They can engage in leisure activities *after* completing their homework. Too often children dawdle and avoid doing homework during the evening when they are less able to focus their attention on the task.

4. If homework seems to take too much time (more than an hour for the elementary grades and more than two or three hours for the secondary grades), contact the teacher.

In addition to these suggestions, parents may find the advice of school psychologists Joan and Albert Hodapp helpful. Their article, "ABC's of Homework: Tips for Parents," appeared in *Interventions in the Clinic and School* (May 1991). The ABC's they discuss are

- **A**ttitude: Communicate a positive attitude toward school and learning to children.
- **B**reaks: Pace and space learning over time to maximize retention and stamina.
- **C**hoice: Let the child select what he or she will work on first and how he or she will study.
- **D**irections: Read the directions carefully. If necessary, reword them for your child.
- **E**ncouragement: Frequently comment positively on your child's effort, neatness, or accuracy.
- **F**urnishings: Suitable lighting, seating, and supplies maximize the likelihood that your child will be comfortable and oriented toward the task.
- **G**ames: Drilling basic concepts can be made more enjoyable through games. Making activities fun increases your child's interest and attention span.

- **H**abits: Set up a routine patter for doing homework—in the same place, at the same time—to build good study habits.
- **I**ncentives: Initially, your child may need some small rewards for building consistent study habits. For example, try stickers, baseball cards, or extra privileges.
- **J**oy: Don't forget that learning should be fun. Relate hard subjects to your child's special interest.
- **K**eys: Remember, certain study habits are the keys to mastery—frequent review, practice over time, and short intense study periods.
- **L**earning Rate: Remember, each child learns at his or her own rate and way. Help your child to find his or her best strategies.
- **M**emory: Frequent review and practice over time help your child remember better than one long, last-minute study time the night before the test.
- **N**ormal: Make homework part of the routine. Even if your child does not have homework, encourage your child to spend some time reading.
- **O**pportunities: Use everyday activities to let your child practice new skills. Let your child write the grocery list, add up the bill, count the coupons, and so forth.
- **P**raise: Find something to sincerely praise your child for—neatness, effort, accuracy, attitude, improvement, and so forth.
- **Q**uality Time: It is not the quantity of time you spend, but rather the quality of time you spend with your child on his or her homework.
- **R**eading: Encourage leisure reading as much as possible. The only way to improve reading is by reading.
- **S**upplies: Having all the materials handy eliminates interruptions and excuses and reinforces good organizational skills.
- **T**eachers: Don't hesitate to ask the teacher for assistance or suggestions. Some school districts have homework hotlines. If there is a persistent problem, schedule a conference.

- Understanding: Be supportive and patient. Homework can be frustrating to both the parent and the child. Wait until you are both relaxed and well rested. Ask someone else to help you if you are caught in a power struggle or if the subject is a struggle for you too.
- Value: Let your child know how important education is to you and reinforce the importance of good study habits.
- Work: Homework is your child's responsibility. Use Grandma's Rule—first you work, then you play.
- Xxxooo's: Words of praise and encouragement will help your child to persist and build a solid foundation of good study habits and self-confidence.
- You: You are a vital participant in your child's education. Model positive attitudes toward learning, help your child where you can, and get assistance when you need it.
- Zzz's: Well-rested and well-nourished children learn better and can concentrate longer. Plan study time when your child is alert—not the last thing before bedtime.

32

∧∧

TUTORING

Many parents of learning disabled students seek the assistance of a tutor. This is not a decision to be taken lightly. This key explains those factors you should consider when getting a tutor for your child.

Who Should Be Tutored?

Your son is having difficulty mastering his addition facts. Your daughter cannot identify the main idea of a reading passage. Does each need a tutor? Probably not. These challenges may easily be resolved by some individual attention or extra help from your child's teacher (self-contained classroom or resource room).

Most teachers have a designated time throughout the school week when students can see them for extra help. Special education teachers know the strengths and weaknesses of their students and can frequently resolve most sporadic school difficulties without resorting to a tutor.

Tutoring should be reserved for a consistent problem with a subject or skill. Tutoring is also helpful for students who are discouraged by their performance and need someone to help improve their self-confidence as well as their academic skills. A student who puts in a great deal of effort without getting results is also a candidate for tutoring.

A tutor may be able to teach efficient learning strategies such as outlining, and notetaking. This is frequently done in a resource room setting in school. In some cases, however, a student needs additional support.

Parents may seek a tutor when they feel frustrated about working with their child. *In many cases parents should not attempt to teach their children* (in the traditional sense). A parents and child benefit immensely if an objective tutor assists and the parent provides the support that is critical for the child's social and emotional growth. Parents are truly their child's first teacher and will always provide them with values, concepts, and skills. However, this should occur in a natural setting, not in a typical "teaching" dynamic that will only heighten the anxiety of the child and parent. Anxiety decreases the child's performance.

Some parents say they don't know why they waited so long to hire a tutor because now they're so relieved to go back to the normal parent-child relationship.

Selecting a Tutor

Generally speaking, tutoring is not a long-term proposition. It should be employed to address a specific need. You should select a teacher with a license in special education who has recent experience working with a child similar to yours. Also, the tutor should have experience in the content area or skill that will be addressed with your child. Some equally good tutors, who are available at little or no cost, are undergraduate or graduate students in education who are closely supervised by their college professors.

Your child's teacher may recommend a tutor. It is not always in your child's best interest to employ his own teacher as a tutor; in fact, many school districts have policies forbidding such a practice because it may present a disincentive to provide individualized help during the school day. As mentioned, it is perfectly acceptable for the classroom teacher to provide extra help before and after school.

Some tutors advertise their services in local newspapers or on community and library bulletin boards. Although they may be reputable and effective tutors, a more objective way for a parent to find a good special education tutor is to call the local college or university. Speak to a professor in the special education department there and ask for a list of qualified tutors.

If you locate one through another source, you should ask the following questions:

- Are you a certified special education teacher?
- Have you ever tutored before?
- Can you provide recommendations from schools as well as from parents of students you have tutored?

A word of caution about the proliferation of tutoring business franchises: If you plan to employ one of these businesses, inquire about the tests it uses, the qualifications of the staff, and data on the effectiveness of their tutorial services.

Most important with any tutor is his willingness and ability to communicate effectively with school personnel. The instruction delivered in tutorial sessions must be transferred to a child's classroom instruction; if not, the sessions are not the path to take toward improving your child's understanding and performance in school.

What to Do Before Tutoring Begins

Once you have decided that your child needs a tutor and have selected a potential tutor, do the following:

- **Arrange for a preliminary visit.** It doesn't matter how effective the tutor has been, if she doesn't hit it off with your child, the tutoring session will be a waste of time and money.

- **Decide on goals.** After the initial meeting with the tutor you should decide on mutually agreeable goals. These goals should be evaluated at least once per month. If there is no improvement, ask why. If, after two or three months, your child makes no improvement, get a new tutor.
- **Discuss how often your child needs to be tutored.** One, one-hour session a week is usually inadequate. It is much better to provide intense tutoring at the onset.
- **Discuss how often the tutor will contact your child's school.** The tutor should contact your child's school at least once a month but preferably every other week, either through a short phone conversation or a progress checklist. This is crucial for special education students because progress needs to be closely monitored and modified if necessary.
- **Discuss the reinforcement the tutor employs.** Not all children like being tutored. It takes away from their free time. Try to find out what techniques the tutor employs to make the sessions more pleasurable.

33

SUMMER SCHOOL

The summer months are the ideal time to alleviate the pressure children with learning disabilities are under during the school year. Therefore, summer school students should not be subjected to as rigid a schedule as they have during the school year, regardless of the course workload in which they are enrolled.

It is also important for parents to remember that the only purpose of attending summer school is to strengthen particular academic weaknesses in students.

In considering summer school programming for their learning disabled child, parents must be the ultimate decision-makers. A child may not wish to attend, but it is the responsibility of the child's parents in conjunction with the child's school personnel to make the appropriate decision for him. Once the student is enrolled in summer school, parents should reinforce his efforts and make his experience as pleasurable as possible.

Recent budget cuts in schools throughout the country have had an impact on the availability of summer school programs for students with learning disabilities. Most children and adolescents with learning disabilities do not have a 12-month program listed on their IEP. Parents have relied on the goodwill of school districts to provide such programs, but due to economic changes this is not always possible.

When a summer school program is not offered, parents can do many things to enhance learning outside of the school setting during this period. Some parents wonder how they can fill their summer with meaningful activities. The following suggestions and activities will help you occupy and enrich their summer days.

Keeping a Schedule

While free time is one of the benefits of a summer vacation, it can also cause major problems. It is very difficult for some students to go from a structured school day to a day that lacks structure. Therefore, you might set up a home schedule, at least during the first few weeks. Obtain a schedule from school. You don't have to follow this exactly, but you can approximate the schedule at home with planned activities in the morning, for example. Afternoons can be more flexible. Parents that have done this report that the transition from school to vacation is more smooth.

Many students flourish during the summer. Without a schedule and homework assignments, they can unwind and sometimes behave better than they do during the school year. Parents who feel more relaxed at this time of year most likely convey this to their children. No matter how relaxed the family is, learning can take place every day of the summer.

Take Trips to Learn

When going on trips, vacations, or just a drive to the beach point out interesting landmarks, discuss the environment or otherwise engage your child in conversation. Summer trips do not have to be costly or long excursions; think of them as field trips that can increase your child's knowledge and vocabulary.

One parent took her children to a different part of their county one morning a week. They asked their local library for reading materials on points of interest. Prior to the trip they read about the places, so that when they visited them, the children were familiar with the things they saw. The children took pictures and made books with them by pasting them on construction paper and writing a sentence for each picture. By summer's end they had a wonderful collection of their experiences.

Read All Summer Long

Encourage your child to read on a daily basis in the summer. Have newspapers, magazines, and books around the home. Make frequent trips to the library—it's usually air-conditioned, and may have a summer reading program or book and film schedule. Bring books to the beach and pool. Go to the library and then get ice cream. Do whatever you must to encourage her to read. Most important, read to your child each day.

Sports Provide Learning Time

Many children are interested in sports. A youngster wrote to a well-known baseball player over the summer and they communicated frequently. This culminated in the child receiving tickets to a Mets' game. The child was thrilled with the tickets, and his parents were thrilled with his increased willingness to write. Take swimming lessons, play tennis at the local high school, go for family bicycle rides each day, or engage in other sports or recreation. Remember, they need something to write about, so increase their experiences. Discuss it with them, then write about it.

Let Your Child Help Around the House

There are so many household tasks that can increase your child's skill development and learning. From setting the table to folding laundry and everything in between, include your child in tasks that encourage him to use fine and gross motor skills, problem-solving and decision-making skills. Let children help with the cooking. A good cooking lesson incorporates so many excellent skills that are applicable in school—attending to a task, measuring, knowledge of quantity, change in chemical properties, and so on.

Encourage Hobbies and Interests

Summer is the perfect time to encourage or reinforce a hobby or unique skill. Many special education experts suggest that parents and teachers try to enable a child to become an expert or very competent in one particular area. Some children love to collect information on dinosaurs, others are into baseball cards. Encourage their interests and curiousity.

With all of these suggestions it might seem contradictory to say relax and enjoy your summer, but that is exactly what you should do. Learning occurs in all settings and it can be relaxing and should be enjoyable. All it takes is a little planning.

Part Five

^^^

THE LEARNING DISABLED CHILD IN THE COMMUNITY

Many parents want their children with learning disabilities to participate in a variety of community activities. Unfortunately, their disability prevents them from being fully involved. This doesn't have to be the case. Part Five of this book deals with how a learning disability manifests itself in a child's community activities and ways in which parents can insure successful and fulfilling involvement for their child.

34

∿∿∿

MANIFESTATIONS IN THE COMMUNITY

For many parents of children with learning disabilities the most trying times are not in the school or at home, but rather in the community. They frequently encounter problems with extended family events, extracurricular activities, friendships, or going to restaurants. The reason for this may be that the school and home environments have more structure and there the child's specific strengths and weaknesses are familiar or predictable.

In the community there is less control over a situation. Also, parents don't always realize that the manner in which children respond to particular situations in the community may be directly related to their learning disability. Not every person with a learning disability has difficulty in community activities and relationships, but the underlying academic disorder also manifests itself in nonacademic situations.

For example, children with memory disorders who forget school-related tasks will also fail to remember rules in a neighborhood ballgame or will forget to call back a friend. Students who struggle with handwriting as a result of poor motor control may have trouble in the Boy Scouts when tying knots, or they may get frustrated doing an arts and crafts project at a birthday party. The following guidelines will help make community activities and relationships more positive experiences for children with learning disabilities.

1. *Know Your Child's Strengths and Weaknesses*

Speak to your child's teacher to find out exactly what things your child does well and what areas are of concern. Ask questions that will enable you to understand how the learning disability may affect activities and relationships in the community, such as, "Do you think it's a good idea for Rosa to join an after-school volleyball league?" The teacher should provide you with her opinion about specific activities. It is not unreasonable to solicit advice on these concerns, but remember that it *is* advice, an opinion. You are ultimately free to decide on the experiences you believe will benefit your child.

2. *Select Activities that Focus on Strengths*

You may think that by selecting activities an area of weakness you can encourage your child to improve certain skills. For example, you place your child, who has difficulty with fine motor control, in an origami program, thinking that the practice she gets will improve her fine motor control. On the contrary, the experience will probably be so negative it will only reinforce her feelings of incompetence in this area. Students who have learning disabilities confront failure on a daily basis during the school day. Their activities outside of school should be enjoyable, positive, and provide them with opportunities to succeed, not fail.

3. *Select Small Groups or Individualized Activities*

Most students with learning disabilities are used to small groups or individualized instruction during school. To thrust them into an activity with a large group of children may be overwhelming. Rather than having your child attend a large ice skating class, try a few individual or small group lessons. The cost is not much different and any initial success will give him the confidence he needs to continue to pursue the activity. Small groups and individualized activities reduce competition and comparisons. Your child will only have to do his best, not worry about how others are doing and how he stacks up against them.

4. *Speak to Coaches and Club Leaders about Your Child's Learning Disability*

In order for your child to have successful extracurricular experiences the adults working with them should be fully informed about the learning disability. You may think that telling a coach or club leader about your child will give them a biased view of your child. But most adults who work in a supervisory capacity with children will detect a problem anyway. It is much better for them to know the exact nature of your child's learning disability, rather than have them assume the worst. It also will help your child succeed because the adults can then address her needs.

If you suspect that informing this person will negatively affect the way your child is treated, you are probably better off not having her participate in this particular activity. Coaches, camp counselors, and scout leaders are very receptive to concerns of parents and make attempts to modify activities to meet the needs of children. However, they can only do this if they are informed about the specific needs of your child.

It is also important for your child to see that a learning disability is not something you are ashamed of or try to hide. Being open about the nature of the disability will help your child deal with it more effectively.

5. *Encourage Special Interests and Hobbies*

Few things excite children more than being an expert in a particular area. Having a special interest or hobby allows children to learn more about a subject than most children or adults. There are children with learning disabilities who are experts on origami, rocks, gymnastics, snakes, race cars, baseball cards, and on and on. Adults have to ask *them* for information on these subjects. If they show confidence in a special area of knowledge like this, their competence will spill over into their school life, where the teacher can reinforce this interest.

Interests and hobbies don't just emerge. They are fostered by parents who give their children information through books, magazines, tapes, discussions, and through taking them on trips to parks, zoos, museums, and other places of interest. A child who visited a Civil War battlefield became incredibly interested in the Civil War and started to listen to tapes, view programs, and eventually read about it. He now knows more about it than most adults! He is proud to have a reputation for this in his school, where teachers sometimes seek him out with questions.

6. *Reinforce Effort*

Sometimes children enjoy a particular activity although they are not good at it. What do you do? Do you tell them not to join the soccer team because they are not well coordinated? Or should they avoid the Cub Scouts because they become overwhelmed in large groups? One way to deal with the issue is to reinforce effort. Praise your child and his efforts, not necessarily the end result. He may never meet your or his expectations, but he'll be more apt to succeed if his efforts are rewarded. Don't wait for him to reach some preconceived level of achievement—he may never reach it. But if you appreciate and praise small successes he may achieve more than you'd expect.

7. *Seek Programs Designed for Children and Adolescents with Learning Disabilities*

You may discover that despite your best efforts there are some activities your child is having considerable difficulty with because of the coach, leader, or program itself. In this case, consult with the teacher to see if there are programs designed specifically for students with learning disabilities. Also contact national, state, and local professional organizations (See Appendix A, Resources for Parents) that may sponsor such activities. Finally, you might ask your school district about the possibility of starting some after school activities for students with learning disabilities.

8. *Ask Your Child What Activities She wants to Participate In*

This advice seems simple, but too often we forget the obvious. A child will be more interested in participating in something she enjoys. Discuss any potential obstacles and how they can be overcome. Most important, if it doesn't work out, allow your child to withdraw.

35

EXTRACURRICULAR ACTIVITIES

E xtracurricular activities can provide wonderful experiences for children with learning disabilities. They can also be sources of painful, unsuccessful experiences. Therefore, it is critical that parents give a great deal of thought before their child's involvement. As previously noted, parents must be aware of their child's strengths and weaknesses and know how the learning disability manifests itself in the home and the community. Speak to your child's teacher if you are not sure or seek the advice of a professional in the field of learning disabilities.

Activities in School

For some children, extracurricular activities are the main reason they go to school. The number of activities tends to increase in higher grades. In the elementary years students may have opportunities to work on a school newspaper, be a member of the band or chorus, and participate in a club, such as the science club or the math club. In some school districts there are extensive after school activities that are not necessarily school related. For example, there are school districts where the P.T.A. runs cooking classes, computer classes, and aerobic classes from 3 to 5 p.m. Some are taught by teachers, but most are not. Although these activities are related to school they are not directly related. As students progress through the school years the number of activities can become endless and overwhelming for some students. Students throughout middle school and junior and senior high school may have a wide variety of sports—group (football, soccer) and individual (horseback riding, gymnastics)—to participate in, as well as a host of service organizations, political clubs, subject matter clubs (spanish club, french club, math club), the debate team, forensics, the school newspaper, and so on.

Participation in sports must be well thought out. It's a good idea to get children involved in a sport when they are young because rules are simplified and competition is usually not as fierce. Also, during the early years children's skill levels vary much more, so your child will have ample opportunity to learn the basics of a sport. In addition, there is usually far greater opportunity to practice during this age.

Before enrolling in a sport, it is crucial that you speak to the coach. It is helpful to explain the nature of your child's learning disability to the coach, providing examples of the way it might be manifested in this sport. You may also want to share some things that you do that are successful in dealing with your child's behavior. Most coaches truly care for children—often volunteering countless hours—and are willing to help when parents inform them.

Sports offer wonderful experiences for physical activity and social interaction if they are appropriate for the child or adolescent. Be careful not to select sports that could lead to injury if your child's disability interferes with the activity. Parents need to consider their child's behavior and the demands of a particular sport and decide if it is a good match. Despite pressure to be athletic, children are not always interested or motivated to participate in sports, and so other activities should be tried.

A distinction should be made between competence and interest. Some clubs, such as the math club, may be based on a level of competence, not merely interest in math. Inquire before having your child sign up only to be embarrassed by his inability to perform like the other club members. Participation in a band is encouraged because the instruction tends to be individualized. Obviously, it is not appropriate for every child with a learning disability—especially if she has difficulty with auditory perception—but too often they are not even given the opportunity. It is very important that parents ensure that their children are provided with these opportunities, as they are an integral part of school.

Activities Outside the School

The list of activities outside of school is endless. There are clubs such as 4-H, Cub Scouts, Brownies, Girl Scouts, and Boy Scouts. The type of club and level of participation cannot be left to chance. When you are deciding upon a particular club, discuss the types of activities the children typically engage in. Are they of interest to your child? Find out how many children are enrolled in the club. The Cub Scouts may sound like a wonderful notion, but the groups may be too large for your child. Inquire about the rules of the club. In some clubs the rules are so extensive that they would challenge any child, not to mention a child with a learning disability. Some clubs spend a lot of time in lectures, while others have greater opportunities for hands-on activities.

Once you narrow down the choices, let your child attend a meeting on a trial basis in order to see if she enjoys the club. The deciding factor will probably be the leader. You should feel comfortable not only with his expertise but with the manner in which he treats children. Go with your instincts if you feel good about him. Provide him with adequate information and give him a few effective techniques for dealing with your child.

Some clubs are geared specifically for children with special needs. For example, there are Brownie, Cub Scout, Boy Scout, and Girl Scout groups just for students with learning disabilities. In general, though most children with learning disabilities can be accommodated in a club for nondisabled children.

Parents can also encourage hobbies and special talent or interest. Hobbies don't just emerge, they must be fostered. Parents must expose their children to a wide variety of experiences and reinforce their interests.

Encouraging Hobbies

A hobby can develop a unique competence that is often hard to find in school or extracurricular activities. If you find it impossible to come up with a hobby that is of interest to your child, ask her teacher for ideas. There are many different activities that children engage in during a school day. Perhaps the teacher has noticed your child's particular interest in some of them, or one in which she has demonstrated competence. Also check with the special subject teachers—art, music, physical education, and computers. Although it is not vital that your child have a hobby, it can do wonders for her self-esteem.

Perhaps even more important than encouraging hobbies is the nurturing of a special talent a child may possess. You might solicit the input of teachers or, if your child has been enrolled in classes such as art, gymnastics, or the like, you might inquire about exploring more advanced levels of one of these courses in which your child demonstrates talent.

It takes an extraordinary time and energy to travel to special places, to seek special events, to balance talents with other activities, but it is necessary if the talents are to emerge. There is a youngster who is an exceptionally good gymnast. She has far exceeded the skill level of her local gymnastic class, so her parents drive her (three times a week) to a special gymnastic academy in order for her to further develop this talent. The student's time must be carefully managed so that she completes homework and attends to other demands.

Not all children have special talents. A child should never be pressured to take lessons in something or be forced to excel. Being forced can make learning or developing skills a negative process. If you simply expose your child to a wide variety of activities at an early age she will have many opportunities for hobbies to develop. When an interest or talent does emerge it should be encouraged.

36

~~~~~~

FRIENDS

Social development researcher Doreen Kronich points out the difficulty a learning disabled individual might encounter with the simple task of inviting a friend to join him at the movies. He would have to (1) determine which movies are playing and decide which ones he would like to see; (2) determine who is likely to want to see that type of movie and who would consider spending time with him; (3) find out where the movie is playing, how to travel there and back, and how long the journey will take; (4) decide whether to meet the friend at the movie or travel together and where the initial meeting will take place; (5) determine the cost of movie, transportation, and perhaps a snack, and where the money will come from; (6) decide whether to invite the friend to his house or to a restaurant before or after the film and, if so, whether it should be for a meal or a snack or other activity and the timing.

Other more complex interactions can obviously be more difficult. These skills cannot be learned merely through observation or admonishments. Rather, they must be taught with the same vigor that academic skills are taught. In fact, many professionals believe that the lack of interpersonal skills in learning disabled students may be more devastating over time than academic deficiencies.

Parents sometimes purchase books on social skill training and developing friendships only to become more frustrated. It helps if the child's teacher can discuss her social interaction strengths and weaknesses with the parents. Social interaction skill building should also be included on the IEP. In come cases children may need the help of a professional who can provide individual training in social skill development or small group interaction.

Parents can assist in the development of friendships by identifying activities that provide structure and reinforcement. If you have children over the house for a play date, try to structure the activity initially to insure success. You may have other children who can play with friends without being supervised. This will probably not be the case with your learning disabled child. Too often play dates disintegrate with the friend leaving and the parent reprimanding the child and asking him, "How do you expect to have friends when you act that way?"

There are things a parent can do that will help in developing friendships.

Help Your Child Fit In

Notice how your child's peers dress, what styles are "in" or "out," how they bring their books to school, and what they wear outside of school. Your child doesn't always have to conform and you needn't buy every item of popular clothing or accessories. Just be sensitive so that your child does not look awkward or very different from others.

One child wanted a specific type of shorts for school and his parents didn't understand the importance of them. Finally, they gave in. The child came home from school beaming with joy that some of his classmates commented on his shorts. When children feel they are perceived as members of the group, their social skills can be boosted. "Fitting in" is crucial at certain ages, especially during the middle school years.

Teach the Importance of Eye Contact

Children that have limited ability to attend often appear bored or uninterested because they don't make eye contact with others. Many people find it terribly disconcerting when you are having a conversation and the individual doesn't look at you. Early on you can reinforce good eye contact and listening behavior. This should be done through praise, not verbal reprimands.

Enable Your Child to Observe Facial Expressions and Body Language

Due to social and perceptual deficits or other unknown reasons children and adolescents with learning disabilities have trouble identifying the feelings of others represented by their facial expressions and body language. There are numerous ways to make them aware of this through observation of real life situations, as well as through TV, movies, and books. You don't have to make every opportunity a lesson, but casually note expressions and how feelings are conveyed physically.

Be a Good Role Model

Share your experiences of making friends with your child. Explain how you select friends, how you initiate a conversation, how you interpret verbal and nonverbal cues, what is appropriate to share with friends and what is not. The more you discuss your actions and behavior the more likely your child will pick up on some aspects of this social skill.

Making friends—it seems so simple, yet for many individuals with learning disabilities it is a problem that persists for years. It must be addressed in a systematic manner, the same as any other skill. It should be taught at school through the IEP and reinforced at home. In some cases, especially for students in the middle and high school years, parents may need to seek the help of a professional outside of the school setting for counseling or specific social skill training.

37

~~~~~~

WORKING AFTER SCHOOL

It is not unusual for adolescents to work after school or during the summer months. However, due to the availability of part-time jobs in fast food restaurants and the like, many school officials complain that students work too many hours, leaving little time for study. Some students need to work for financial reasons, but some surveys suggest that many students work to accumulate the trappings of a teenage lifestyle—clothing, cars, stereos, and so on.

Barring economic need, an adolescent with learning disabilities should limit the number of hours of after school employment. There are benefits of a job, such as learning how to accept and handle responsibilities, receiving feedback from coworkers and supervisors, and experiencing the world of work. However, the amount of time and the physical energy that goes into such employment may leave little time for school-related activities and studying.

Perhaps you have come up with the ideal work situation that allows for age-appropriate adolescent activities, school activities, and homework. There are still a number of things you need to consider when contemplating after school or summer employment for your learning disabled adolescent.

Let Employers Know Your Child Has a Learning Disability
If you think the employer will treat your child negatively due to the learning disability, then you probably wouldn't want

your child to work there. The employer may become aware of the learning disability and act upon it. It is better to explain as clearly as possible some of the difficulties your child may encounter due to his learning disabilities before he starts a job there.

Some children don't want the boss to know because they would be embarrassed. It is important that students with learning disabilities know exactly what it means to have them and to be advocates for themselves. If they are embarrassed, they need to receive some professional help as soon as possible.

Some parents have asked teachers to speak to prospective employers; and others have provided clear, jargon-free articles on learning disabilities to help the employer understand their child's needs. No matter how you choose to do it, it is important to share as much information as necessary with employers.

Specific Hours vs. "On-Call"

Many youngsters have jobs where they are called that day or the night before and informed of their hours. For students with learning disabilities, this can be disastrous. They need to know in advance so they can organize a schedule. Many students with learning disabilities have organizational difficulties and cannot handle priorities and certain responsibilities. This kind of job only complicates matters. If they cannot have a weekly schedule or set hours look elsewhere.

Do They Receive Training?

In some jobs the training is purely "incidental learning." That is, employees watch and infer what they are supposed to do. Parents of children with learning disabilities know that most skills must be taught directly. Therefore, find out if your child will receive job training and how much. It would be unfair to place a student with a learning disability in a job where the training was minimal or only involved watching someone else perform the tasks and then being alone to cope. This would set such an individual up for failure.

Is the Job a Good Match for Your Child?

Consider the strengths and weaknesses of your child and analyze the demands of the job. If your child's major deficits are in the language arts areas, avoid jobs that require a great deal of reading and writing.

Finding a good match is not always so obvious. There was a young man in a dry cleaning business who was sorting articles, and was unexpectedly required to write up customer tickets (name, address, etc.). It was hard for him to spell names and write them legibly on the ticket. No one on the job knew about his difficulty, and everyone soon thought he had a problem. This situation could have been averted if the learning disability had been explained to his employer in the beginning and if all aspects of the job were explained. Consult with your child's teacher to help make a job decision if you are not sure.

Select a Job that Capitalizes on Strengths

There was a young woman who was very disorganized, had a poor memory, and often missed classes and appointments. Her parents were able to secure a job for her in a field they thought could force her to overcome these problems— sales. Needless to say, she failed miserably. Her deficits could not be overcome by having to confront them on a daily basis. She needed specific strategies to assist her, and on the job was not the place to learn them.

Consider the Social Skills Necessary for the Job

Many adults with learning disabilities can perform the tasks necessary for a specific job, but lack the social skills needed in the work environment. The same may be true for adolescents. Some jobs require little social interaction with peers or the public, but others require a great deal. If this is an area of concern for your child, avoid this type of job until those deficits have been sufficiently addressed.

Your child should not be discouraged from seeking after school or summer employment if she wants to. Many adolescents with learning disabilities perform beautifully on their jobs. In fact, the jobs may well be the most satisfying part of their day when the work goes well. However, an equal number of adolescents have had incredibly negative experiences and view the world of work with fear and anxiety. A little thought and planning can insure positive work experiences.

Part Six

~~~~~~

OTHER CONCERNS

The final part of this book deals with issues that concern many people in the field of learning disabilities. They are explained in order to provide parents with information about these important topics: learning disabilities in urban settings; controversial ways of treating learning disabilities; and issues related to the retention of children with learning disabilities.

38

LEARNING DISABILITIES IN URBAN SETTINGS

L arge urban areas are characterized by cultural and linguistic diversity. Dr. Jacqueline Jones, a research scientist at Educational Testing Service in Princeton, New Jersey, notes that this is both a benefit and a challenge to the educational system. The special education process from referral to classification to placement is greatly confounded by issues of language and culture.

This is particularly true when it comes to students with learning disabilities. In the last part of the definition of learning disabilities, often referred to as the exclusionary clause, it states that "cultural differences" or "economic disadvantages" cannot be the primary factor in the diagnosis of a learning disability. For many, this means children in urban settings are not eligible for classification as learning disabled.

However, children in urban settings have received special education services. In a study by Research for Better Schools in 1986, it was noted that the median (mid-point) of new referrals of 28 large urban school districts was 2,358, with New York City reporting the highest at 33,855. Most of these who are referred will eventually be classified as special education students.

The real concern has been with the racial and ethnic breakdown of the referrals. It has been widely documented that a disproportionate number of minority group students are in the special education system. This finding was first reported in the area of mental retardation. However, recent research points to the same finding in the field of learning disabilities. Some suggest that in urban areas, learning disabilities—the fastest growing area of special education—is becoming a dumping ground category for those students who are difficult to teach.

Parents in urban areas need to beware if their child is referred for special education services. Ask the following questions:

- What is the racial/ethnic breakdown of special education in your district?
- What tests are being used in the evaluation?
- Are the tests sensitive to the needs of cultural and linguistic differences?
- Are the examiners competent to evaluate children from cultural and linguistic minorities?
- What percentage of students who are referred are eventually classified in special education.
- What has been done in the regular classroom prior to referral?

If you are a member of a cultural or linguistic minority group in America, you should be even more cautious. For example, in New York City African-American children were 50 percent more likely to be referred for special education during their first and second years of school than Caucasian students. And when patterns of referrals to special education are expanded to include all school-age students, there is a 96 percent chance that teachers refer African-American or Hispanic students more than Caucasian students.

The referral process in urban settings obviously needs to be reexamined. Many schools throughout the country have recognized the problem and are beginning to address it. Some schools have provided staff with workshops, courses, and other information to make them more aware of the needs of a culturally and linguistically diverse population. Teacher training programs are addressing the issue by incorporating competency tests related to this problem into their curriculum. And perhaps most important, a great deal of work is being undertaken in the area of assessment in order to devise more equitable ways to evaluate student performance.

In summary, the number of students referred for special education services in urban settings is staggering. More troubling is the high rate of referrals for culturally and linguistically diverse students. While this is alarming it should be reassuring to parents in urban areas that the problem is out in the open. For years it was well-known in the professional community, but not widely known by the public. However, recent reports in newspapers and on TV have addressed the issue.

Parents need to be informed in order to be advocates for their children. Ask questions, speak to professionals, join parent-teacher organizations, or get involved as a parent member of the Council for Exceptional Children (a special education organization that has been particularly active on this issue).

39

CONTROVERSIAL TREATMENTS

The field of learning disabilities appears to be plagued by popular treatments that are not supported by research. Parents of children with learning disabilities are particularly vulnerable to undocumented claims of success, and thus they need to be cautious. Three approaches that are particularly popular now are (1) Scotopic Sensitivity training, (2) visual Training, and (3) the Feingold Diet.

Scotopic Sensitivity Training

This approach was developed by Dr. Helen Irlen, a psychologist, who uses colored lenses to correct for light sensitivity that she suggests interferes with learning. Her approach was featured a few years ago on *60 Minutes* and its popularity has increased tremendously. The Irlen Institute for Perceptual and Learning Disabilities has branches in many cities throughout the United States and screens students for scotopic sensitivity syndrome (SSS). The characteristics of students with SSS are very broad. They include headaches, burning or itchy eyes, dry eyes, fatigue, and words doubling, moving, looking fuzzy, and disappearing.

Dr. Irlen suggests these individuals may rub their eyes, blink excessively, squint, open their eyes wide, shade the page, hold the reading material close to their eyes, cover one eye, read word by word, or use a finger to hold their place.

Once it is determined that the individual responds well to particular colored lenses they are advised to get such glasses.

To date there are no empirical studies to support this approach. The results provided so far are from individual case studies or testimonials from individual clients. Until this treatment can be supported by impartial, scientific evidence it cannot be recommended to parents of children with learning disabilities.

Visual Training

Characteristics of students whose visual difficulties affect learning may include: moving ahead when reading, using a finger to keep place, skipping lines, skipping words, ignoring punctuation, difficulty coloring a ball, short attention span, fatigue when reading, reads only short books, or trouble with reading comprehension. Once the diagnosis has been made students receive training (from an optometrist) in the movements of the eye and eye-hand coordination.

Most experts in the field of learning disabilities do not believe that reading is merely a visual task and learning disabilities are not caused by visual defects. Therefore, visual training cannot cure a learning disability as proponents of this approach suggest. And, as is the case with Scotopic Sensitivity Training, there is no credible evidence to suggest that visual training works.

There is a long history of controversy surrounding visual training. A statement policy on learning disabilities, dyslexia, and vision approved in 1992 by the American Academy of Pediatrics, the American Association for Pediatric Ophthalmology and Strabismus, and the American Academy of Ophthalmology, notes that there is no known eye or visual cause for dyslexia and learning disabilities, and no effective visual treatment.

Feingold Diet

In 1975, Benjamin Feingold, M.D., published his best-selling book, *Why Your Child Is Hyperactive*. His theory, based on his clinical observations as an allergist, was that food additives cause hyperactivity and learning disorders. His solution was simple—eliminate food additives. Dr. Feingold was a charismatic and powerful speaker, and parents responded to him. At the time he proposed his diet many people were concerned about the food they ate and how it affected them. Before long there were Feingold Associations cropping up throughout the United States. The diet listed here shows foods he recommends eliminating.

Group 1

Green pepper	Peaches
Nectarines	Tangerines
Oranges	All teas
Plums and prunes	Tomatoes

Group 2

Foods containing artificial flavors

Baked goods, except bread	Ice cream
Beverages	Condiments
Candy	Gelatin
Chewing gum	Preserves

Group 3

Foods containing artificial colors

Blues #1 and #2, Green #3, Reds #3 and #40, and Yellows #5 and #6. Two food colors are limited in use to one product each: Orange B for hot dogs and Citrus Red #2 for orange skin.

Group 4

Foods containing preservatives

Butylated hydroxy toluene (BHT)
Butylated hydroxy anisole (BHA)

Group 5

Foods containing natural salicylates

Almonds	Coffee
Apples	Cucumber and pickles
Apricots	Currants
Cherries	Grapes and raisins
Cloves	

Although parents reported remarkable success with the diet, the scientific community responded with skepticism. Throughout the years since the diet was introduced there has been considerable debate over its effectiveness. Parents say it works; researchers say there is little, if any, support. Studies have been criticized for being poorly executed, and parents have been criticized for seeking quick cures. Well-controlled studies have not found that food additives cause hyperactivity in 98 to 99 percent of the children. Why it seems to work for the other 1 to 2 percent is not clear.

Other approaches will no doubt come along that will be equally controversial. Contact a local college or university and speak to a faculty member in the special education department. They will be up to date on the latest approaches and can provide you with nonbiased information. You can also write or call one of the professional organizations listed in Appendix A.

Too many parents that have spent considerable time and money trying to help their children by employing these unfounded approaches only to be very disappointed in the results. They have also lost valuable time that could have been spent on traditional, scientifically documented treatments.

40

RETENTION

I f a student is having difficulty in school, especially in the
early grades, simply retaining him, or having him repeat the
grade, will not in most cases solve the problem. Rather, by
implementing an approach that allows for adequate assessment of students and a flexible, realistic curriculum, the system
should be able to accommodate a variety of individual differences in the classroom.

Should a child be retained if he is consistently having
difficulty in all areas of school, is considerably below the
performance level of all other students, and is recommended
for retention by a professional who has considered a variety of
resources?

Most parents might say yes. Yet cases where there is such
uniformity of performance and opinion are rare. And even if
this were the case, parents still need to pursue additional
activities prior to making their decision on retention.

Making the Right Grade-Placement Decision

For parents facing the retention dilemma, here are some
suggestions to consider prior to finalizing their position:

1. What is the basis for retention? Is it social, academic,
   or developmental?
2. How far below grade expectations is the child? How
   does this compare to other members of her class?
3. What are the sources of information—standardized
   test scores, individual evaluations by an independent
   source, such as a local university, anecdotal reports,

or teacher recommendations? Have other professionals in the school (psychologist, social worker, principal) observed the child?

4. Is there consensus among the professionals about retention?

5. Is the child's performance consistent or has her performance only recently been brought to attention?

6. Have the parents visited their child's current class and the class that she will attend in the upcoming school year?

7. Have the parents spoken to school personnel individually about their child?

8. What is the number of children presently being retained by her particular school, and how have retained children performed in subsequent years?

9. How does the child feel about the decision?

Students with learning disabilities need to be identified at an early age and provided with an appropriate educational program. Merely having them repeat classes or grades is not going to meet their needs or improve them. Parents need to explore this approach with school personnel thoroughly before coming to a decision. Much research does not support retention for any youngster. In the case of a child with a learning disability it may only delay appropriate interventions.

QUESTIONS AND ANSWERS

What do I do if I think my child has a learning disability?

Contact your child's teacher and the director of special education and request an evaluation.

What causes a learning disability?

There are many factors such as central nervous system disorders and genetic factors that have been suggested as causes of a learning disability, but no one cause has been determined.

Do children outgrow a learning disability?

No. However, with the right treatment they can learn strategies to compensate for their disability.

Can students with learning disabilities go to college?

Yes. In fact there are hundreds of colleges throughout the United States that have programs specifically for students with learning disabilities.

Do all children with learning disabilities have Attention Deficit Disorder (ADD)?

No. About one-third of all children classified as learning disabled also have Attention Deficit Disorder.

Is one reading approach more effective for students with learning disabilities?

To date there is not enough research to suggest one approach is better than another. The most effective approach is one that teaches with a focus on the students' strengths while remediating the weakness.

Should students with learning disabilities be educated in the regular classroom?

Most students with learning disabilities are educated in regular classrooms with support (usually the resource room). However, the individual needs of the student must be considered when making a decision about class placement.

Are students with learning disabilities classified as special education students?

Yes. According to Public Law 94-142 and more recently IDEA (Individuals with Disabilities Act) students who are eligible for classification as learning disabled are considered special education students.

Does the label "learning disabled" stay on students' school records?

Upon completion of high school or age 21 all information related to the disability is removed. All that remains are name, address, phone number, and a listing of courses taken.

How many students are classified as learning disabled?

While it may appear to be a very popular classification, only about 3 to 5 percent of school-aged children are classified as learning disabled.

GLOSSARY

Attention deficit disorder (ADD) difficulty in concentrating and staying on task. It may or may not also include hyperactivity.

Attention deficit hyperactivity disorder (ADHD) difficulty in concentrating and staying on task. Hyperactivity causes part of the attention deficit.

Central nervous system dysfunction a learning disorder caused by an impairment in brain functions.

Curriculum-based assessment ongoing assessment of student performance on specific curriculum tasks.

Expressive language the ability to put your ideas into words.

Feingold diet a diet that eliminates artificial food additives in an attempt to control hyperactivity.

Inclusion a philosophy proposing that all students with special educational needs be educated in the regular classroom.

Individualized Education Program (IEP) a written plan that describes the special education services a student will receive.

Learning disability a term used to describe children with average intelligence who are not achieving up to potential. It is presumed to be due to a central nervous system dysfunction.

Mainstreaming placing children with disabilities within the regular classroom.

Perception how you interpret information.

Receptive language your understanding of language.

Selective attention the ability to pay attention to certain parts of a task.

Social perception how you interpret social situations.

Social skills skills necessary to meet the basic demands of everyday life.

Task analysis breaking a task into small parts.

Visual training the attempt to improve reading by training visual skills.

Appendix A

~~~~~~

RESOURCES FOR PARENTS

Organizations

The organizations listed here provide information and support for parents of children with learning disabilities. Most were founded through the collaboration of professionals in the field and parents, and have national, state, and local chapters.

> Council for Exceptional Children
> Division for Learning Disabilities
> 1920 Association Drive
> Reston, VA 22091
> (703) 620-3666

> Council for Learning Disabilities
> P.O. Box 40303
> Overland Park, KS 66204
> (713) 492-8755

> Learning Disability Association of America
> 4156 Library Road
> Pittsburgh, PA 15234
> (412) 341-1515

National Center for Learning Disabilities
99 Park Avenue/Sixth Floor
New York, NY 10016
(212) 670-7219

Orton Dyslexia Society
724 York Road
Baltimore, MD 21204
(301) 296-0232

Books

Parents can also benefit from reading about learning disabilities in the following books.

Buzenberg, A. *Learning Disabilities: Your Child and You: Handbook for Parents*. Chapel Hill, NC: LDA of North Carolina, 1990.

Lavoie, R.D. *F.A.T. City*. Washington, D.C.: Greater Washington Educational Telecommunications, Inc., 1990. Guides and Video.

McCarney, S., Stephen, B., and Bauer, A. *The Parents Guide to Learning Disabilities*. Columbus, OH: Hawthorne Educational Services, 1991.

Silver, L.B. *The Misunderstood Child. A Guide for Parents of Learning Disabled Children*, 2nd Ed. Blue Ridge Summit, PA: TAB Books, 1992.

Smith, S.L. *Succeeding Against All Odds: Strategies and Insights from the Learning Disabled*. J.P. Tarchen, Inc., 1992.

Swenson, S.S. and Weisberg, P.G. *Questions and Answers About Learning Disabilities: The Learning Disabled, Their Parents and Professionals Speak Out*. Austin, TX: PRO-ED, 1992.

Waldbrown, F.H. *So Your Child Has a Learning Problem, Now What?: A Book for Parents and Teachers*. Brandon, VT: Clinical Psychology Pub. Co., 1990.

Parents as well as siblings can also learn a great deal by reading books that are written for children and adolescents with learning disabilities. You may also want to read some of the books written for professionals.

Books for Children with Learning Disabilities about Learning Disabilities

Cummings, R. and Fisher, G. *The Survival Guide for Teenagers with Learning Disabilities.* William Gladden Foundation, 1994.

Dwyer, K.M. *What Do You Mean I Have a Learning Disability?* NY: Walker & Co., 1991.

Fisher, G. and Cummings, R. *The Survival Guide for Kids with Learning Disabilities.* Minneapolis, MN: Free Spirit, 1991.

Fullen, D. *Lessons Learned: Students with Learning Disabilities Share What They've Learned About Life & Learning.* Mountain Books, 1993.

Hayes, Marnell, L. *The Tuned-In, Tuned-On Book About Learning Problems.* Novato, CA: Academic Therapy Publications, 1994.

Levine, M. *Keeping a Head in School: A Student's Book about Learning Abilities and Learning Disabilities.* Cambridge, MA: Educators Publishing Service, Inc., 1991.

Levinson, M. *And Don't Bring Jeremy.* NY: Holt, Rinehart & Winston, 1985.

Roby, C. *When Learning Is Tough: Kids Talk about Learning Disabilities.* Whitman, Albert, & Co., 1993.

Social Skills Programs

ASSET: A Social Skills Program for Adolescents with Learning Disabilities (Research Press). A social skills program based on instruction in learning strategies.

DUSO (Developing Understanding of Self and Others)

(American Guidance Services). Activities and kits to stimulate social and emotional development in children in grades K-4.

Getting Along with Others (Research Press). Teaching students skills for being in group activities.

Skill Streaming the Adolescent: A Structural Learning Approach to Teaching Prosocial Skills (Research Press). Activities for developing social skills in adolescents.

Skill Streaming the Elementary School Child: A Guide for Teaching Prosocial Skills (Research Press). Activities for developing social skills in elementary school children.

Social Skill Instruction for Daily Living (American Guidance Services). Activities for adolescents with learning disabilities.

Social Skills Intervention (American Guidance Services). A social skills program for students with learning disabilities.

The Social Skills Curriculum (American Guidance Services). A curriculum for teaching social skills.

TAD (Toward Affective Development) (American Guidance Services). Group activities, lessons, and materials to stimulate psychological and affective development for students in grades 3 through 6.

The Walker Social Skills Curriculum: The Accepts Program (PRO-ED). Activities for developing social skills within the school curriculum.

Appendix B

〰〰〰〰〰〰〰〰〰〰〰〰〰〰〰〰〰〰〰〰〰〰〰〰〰〰〰〰〰〰〰〰

RESOURCES FOR TEACHERS

Most children with learning disabilities will spend the majority of their school day in a regular classroom setting. Regular educators can provide effective instruction by employing the teaching methods described below.

- plan for small increments of change
- use modeling, prompting, and shaping
- provide for practice, review, and generalization
- use concrete materials before moving to abstract ideas
- provide feedback and reinforcement
- communicate effectively
- evaluate instruction

In addition to these generic competencies, effective teachers recognize that, despite the presence or absence of a disability, students learn in different ways. They are aware that if all students' needs are to be met, they must modify their methods. Modifications can be made by

1. changing how instruction is delivered,
2. changing the student response,
3. changing who delivers instruction,
4. changing the conditions of instruction.

1. **Change how instruction is delivered.** Rather than the typical verbal lecture-discussion model you may want to use various **media presentations**, such as films, filmstrips,

slides, tape recordings, overhead transparencies, and opaque projectors. Teaching machines, such as the "Language Master," "Little Professor," and "Speak and Spell," employ specific instructional programs for academic skill acquisition.

Teachers should also consider the use of **learning centers** throughout the classroom. These centers can be used as primary or supplementary means of instruction. Good learning centers consist of clearly stated objectives, specific directions, samples of the work to be completed, a schedule for students, and a record-keeping procedure.

Programmed instruction is another alternative to the typical teacher-student interaction. Programmed materials provide repetitive instruction in small increments to students. The student usually is provided with immediate feedback, thereby reducing failure.

Many students with learning or behavioral problems learn best through "experimental learning," that is, they learn best by doing. The of concrete materials, real-life experiences, role playing, simulations, and problem solving are examples of methods that change the manner in which instruction is being delivered.

A **parallel alternative curriculum** allows the student who is functioning below grade level in a particular subject to acquire the same material in that subject that his peers are getting. Texts may be put on audio tape; the complexity of a book may be reduced by adapting it (this is very time consuming!); books can be provided that cover the same content, written on a lower level (contact the publisher of your current text) or oral presentations instead of written material may be used, such as films and filmstrips, as well as the audio tape previously mentioned.

2. Change the student response

- tape answers
- dictate answers
- type answers
- do projects
- use graph paper to align work
- provide cues for recall
- use a consistent format

3. **Change who delivers instruction.** Teachers do not have to be the only ones who provide instruction in the classroom. Students can—and do—learn from each other. Peer tutoring and teaching devices can be employed in such a way that students have an opportunity to learn from others. These methods can be coupled with the techniques listed above and should be thought of as a viable option in all classrooms.

4. **Change the conditions of instruction.** Teachers may want to vary the organization of the classroom so that some instruction can be in a large group, some a small group, some by peer tutoring, etc. The "where" of instruction is also important for many students. You can try to provide workspace for students in specific areas of the room or on the perimeter of the group. Some students need study carrels to avoid distraction, while others find such workplaces too confining.

Other effective alternatives for presenting information to students:

- Let students know what you will cover.

    provide background information
    motivate students to learn
    identify topics and tasks
    provide a structured framework for the class period
    clarify required activity

      introduce vocabulary
      state concepts to be learned
      state expected outcome

- Provide a list of sample questions BEFORE to reading assign-ments or lectures.
- Provide written back-up to oral directions and lectures
- Allow good notetakers to use carbon paper to make copies of their notes for problem learners.
- To maintain attention:

      combine visual and auditory presentations
      establish eye contact with students during oral directions and lectures
      write assignments and objectives on the chalkboard
      pause every 6 to 8 minutes during a lecture for questions
      give examples and demonstrations
      review throughout
      summarize at the end of each lesson
      give cues about what is important

Teachers can also benefit from consulting books and journals dealing with students with learning disabilities.

Books

Bender, W.N. (Ed.) *Learning Disabilities: Best Practices for Professionals*. Philadelphia, PA: Butterworth-Heineman, 1993.

Farnham-Diggory, S. *The Learning Disabled Child*. Cambridge, MA: Harvard University Press, 1992.

Hammill, D.D. & Bartel, N.R., *Teaching Students with Learning and Behavior Problems*. (5th Ed.) Boston, MA: Allyn & Bacon, 1990.

Lerner, J.W., *Learning Disabilities: Theories, Diagnosis and Teaching Strategies*. (6th Ed.) Boston, MA: Houghton Mufflin, 1993.

LaVoie, R.D. *Integrating Learning Disabled Students*. East Moline, IL: LinguiSystems, Inc. 1992. Guide and Audio Cassettes.

McNamara, B.E. *The Resource Room: A Guide for Special Educators*. Albany, NY: Sate University of New York Press, 1989.

Meltzer, L.J. (Ed.) *Strategy Assessment and Instruction for Students with Learning Disabilities: From Theory to Practice*. Austin, TX: PRO-ED., 1993.

Mercer, C.R. and Mercer, A. *Teaching Students with Learning Problems* (3rd Ed.). NY: Macmillan, 1993.

Smith, C.R. *Learning Disabilities: The Interaction of Learner, Task and Setting*. (3rd Ed.) Boston, MA: Allyn & Bacon, 1994.

Journals

Interventions in the Clinic and Classroom

Journal of Learning Disabilities

Learning Disability Quarterly

Teaching Exceptional Children

Appendix C

^^

RESOURCES FOR SIBLINGS

Newsletters

The National Association of Sibling Programs Newsletter. A newsletter with useful information and activities related to workshops throughout the country for siblings. Contact:

> Sibling Support Project
> Children's Hospital and Medical Center
> Seattle, WA 98002

The Sibling Information Network Newsletter. Published quarterly, it provides information for and about siblings of people with disabilities. Contact:

> Sibling Information Network
> The A.J. Pappanikou Center on
> Special Educational Rehabilitation:
> a University Affiliated Program
> Main Office
> 991 Main St.
> East Hartford, CT 06108

Books

Meyer, D.J., Vadascy, P.F. & Kewell, R.R. *Living with a Brother or Sister with Special Needs.* Seattle, Washington: University of Washington Press, 1985. This book is most appropriate for siblings ages 8 through 13. It discusses a variety of disabilities and presents strategies that will assist siblings in expressing their feelings.

Sullivan, M.B., Brightman, J. & Blatt, J. *Feeling Free.* Reading, Massachusetts: Addison-Wesley, 1979.

An activity book with short stories and accounts written by children with learning problems or physical disabilities.

Siblings benefit from reading books geared toward their brothers or sisters who have a learning disability. There are also sections in the books for parents that are appropriate for siblings (see Appendix A).

Products

Skills for Special Sibs: Living with Your Handicapped Brother or Sister. (1980). VHF Video, color, 13 minutes.

This tape is appropriate for the elementary level child and provides a wide variety of skills for siblings, such as praising, ignoring, expressing anger, that are useful in sibling interaction. It is distributed by

> Child Development Division
> Dept. of Pediatrics/Division of Biomedical
>   Communication
> University of Texas Medical Branch at Galveston
> Galveston, TX 77550

INDEX